COOL CAREERS WITHOUT COLLEGE
FOR PEOPLE WHO ARE REALLY GOOD AT
SCIENCE & MATH

NEW

COOL CAREERS WITHOUT COLLEGE
FOR PEOPLE WHO ARE REALLY GOOD AT
SCIENCE & MATH

DANIEL McGUINNESS

ROSEN PUBLISHING®

New York

Published in 2014 by The Rosen Publishing Group, Inc.
29 East 21st Street, New York, NY 10010

First Edition

Library of Congress Cataloging-in-Publication Data

McGuinness, Daniel.
Cool careers without college for people who are really good at science and math/ Daniel McGuinness.—First edition.
    pages cm.—(New cool careers without college)
Includes bibliographical references and index.
ISBN 978-1-4777-1823-0 (library binding)
1. Science—Vocational guidance—Juvenile literature. 2. Mathematics— Vocational guidance—Juvenile literature. I. Title.
Q147.M34 2014
502.3—dc23
                                                                2013010942

Manufactured in the United States of America

CPSIA Compliance Information: Batch #W14YA: For further information, contact Rosen Publishing, New York, New York, at 1-800-237-9932.
A portion of the material in this book has been derived from *Cool Careers Without College for Math and Science Wizards* by Betty Burnett.

CONTENTS

INTRODUCTION

Modern science fascinates many young people. Reports of medical breakthroughs, scientific expeditions in foreign countries, and the "green" environmental movement excite them. They want to take part, perhaps as a career.

Mathematics appeals to others. They love to solve problems and observe how math is used in different tasks and activities of everyday life. Some of these students, including science-minded teenagers, wonder if their special interests and skills could lead to a vocation.

You might be one of them—and you might feel discouraged by career prospects. College degrees are required for most science and math professions. Some jobs call for years of advanced study. With economic uncertainty and rapid changes in society, how can college students be sure of finding a good job? The thriving career that they begin preparing for today may by dying out four years from now.

The great news is that for many jobs in science and math, you don't need a college education. You may be able to find excellent employment soon after high school. You can learn on the job. You immediately begin to acquire a

A teacher monitors students performing chemical experiments. Students interested in science-related careers should learn as much as they can while in junior high and high school.

job quality that, in some career fields, is even more important than a college degree: experience.

Science and math wizards are always curious. To them, a problem is not a cause for worry or dread. It's a challenge, and they are ready to look for a solution. Are you like that? Is "What if?" one of your favorite questions? When you watch a science-fiction movie, are you especially interested in how the special effects were done? Are you excited by reports of abnormal occurrences—and eager to find explanations?

Science and math types have a "show me" attitude. They want proof. They love to work with gadgets, numbers, and formulas. They may not be as good with social skills as they are with gizmos and calculations. Sometimes they take pride in solving problems on their own, but they also like to conduct research and experiments with others on a team.

The scientific method of problem solving is basically simple. Scientists begin by asking a question. For example: Why doesn't this computer work? They come up with a tentative answer: It isn't plugged in. They test their theory by plugging in the computer and flipping the power switch. If the computer boots up, they were correct. If not, they were wrong. They start over with another theory to test.

There are four main fields of science. Mathematics is the science of numbers. Mathematicians work with numerical combinations, operations, and formulas. Some areas of mathematics are abstract. Some involve measuring distance, space, mass, speed, and time.

Physics deals with matter, energy, and how those forces are related. Physical scientists study the physical properties and processes of objects and systems.

Chemistry is the study of all types of substances—what's in them, how they are put together, and how they interact and change.

Biology is the study of plants and animals. Some biologists study the life processes of a particular organism. Some study how life-forms interact within a local ecosystem. Others study life within a larger environment.

Within each main category of science are divisions and subdivisions. A few of the divisions are:

- Anthropology—The study of people and culture
- Astronomy—The study of stars, planets, and galaxies
- Atmospheric science—The study of the weather and climate
- Biochemistry—The study of the chemistry of living things (combining chemistry and biology)
- Botany—The study of plants
- Geography—The study of landforms and maps
- Geology—The study of the structure of Earth (rocks and minerals)
- Metallurgy—The study of metals
- Oceanography—The study of the oceans
- Psychology—The study of animal and human behavior
- Robotics—The study of automated products
- Zoology—The study of animals

Combined, the different categories of mathematics and other sciences present thousands of career opportunities. Most have one factor in common: they are changing. The science- or math-related job you land today almost certainly will be different in a few years. Expect to learn new job skills.

CHAPTER 1

ASSISTING CIVIL ENGINEERS

Many young people are puzzled by what an engineer does. There are hundreds of types of engineers, yet the term "engineering" sounds vague.

We might think of engineers as "practical scientists" who solve everyday problems. They design, build, and repair things as simple as paperclips, as massive as skyscrapers, and as complex as antilock brakes. Technicians are employed to assist engineers in all fields of engineering.

Civil engineering is a cross between technology and art or architecture. It's the science behind great structures—airports, highways, bridges, dams, and sports domes. Architects design such structures and advise how they should be built. Civil engineers wear hard hats and oversee the construction.

In addition, manufacturers hire engineering teams to build prototypes of new products and test them for safety and reliability.

Civil engineers must understand which ideas will work and which won't before millions of dollars are spent on a building project. Technicians work under their supervision, helping with research and development. Technicians also assist with planning and design. They work with project supervisors.

Among the typical duties of civil engineering technicians are:

- Reviewing project blueprints
- Working with supervisors in planning and evaluating conditions
- Inspecting contractors' work and helping make sure that a project meets construction codes and design specifications
- Developing plans for system installation
- Drafting project reports and keeping activity and data records

Much of the work of engineering technicians is done with computers. They use a variety of software programs, including drawing, data management, and word processing.

ENGINEERING GONE AWRY

Top-quality work is vital in every engineering project, and the role of everyone involved is important. Poor design or construction could endanger people's lives.

The modern Tay Rail Bridge in Dundee, Scotland, is much sturdier and safer than its predecessor, which collapsed in a fierce gale in 1879, killing everyone aboard a train.

One December night in 1879, a train entered the long, curving Tay Rail Bridge to cross the mouth of the River Forth at Dundee, Scotland. A ferocious storm was howling across the water. Winds as high as 71 miles per hour (114 kilometers per hour) were recorded. No one was concerned for safety, though. The new bridge, opened the year before, was considered an engineering marvel.

A railway lineman watched the taillights of the caboose shrink in the distance. Suddenly he saw sparks from the rails. There was a bright flash...then total, eerie darkness.

Daylight revealed not only that the train had gone into the river, but that more than 1,000 yards (914 meters) of the great bridge had been blown down. All seventy-five people aboard the train died.

Inspectors identified several causes of the bridge collapse: flawed design, lack of quality control in the manufacture of certain parts, and inadequate maintenance.

Good came from the tragedy. British government regulators required that bridges in the future be built to withstand greater wind pressure.

Technicians actually perform some of the same tasks as civil engineers, although they are not qualified to supervise work or approve designs. On some projects, they specify materials to use and make cost estimates. Some of their work is done in the engineer's office. Other work is performed at job sites. Technicians often go with engineers to a construction site and then return to the office to help develop a proposal. They work with cost estimators to figure out a budget for the project.

One of the technician's most important tools is computer technology, especially computer-aided design (CAD) software. Using a CAD program, a technician can completely "build" a structure and modify it to suit new ideas and needs as they emerge. As CAD software becomes more sophisticated, technicians must learn to use the upgrades. They input numerical values and calculate formulas to determine details about the materials needed for a project.

The U.S. Bureau of Labor Statistics, in its *Occupational Outlook Handbook*, observes: "Civil engineering technicians learn to use design software that civil engineers typically do not. Thus, those who master it, keep their skills current, and stay abreast of the latest software will likely improve their chances of employment."

Civil engineering technicians have excellent math skills. They also possess critical-thinking skills, allowing them to identify problems as a project progresses and avoid wasting time and money. They must have a mind for solving problems, prioritizing information and tasks, and monitoring projects.

Technicians need good reading and writing skills. They must understand the engineer's plans and designs in order to do their part in completing the project. Often they're expected to write clear, accurate, well-organized project reports.

PREPARING YOURSELF

Candidates for careers as civil engineering technicians should be good students of math and science, especially physics. Most employers prefer applicants who have an associate's degree in engineering technology, but it is not always required; the necessary skills may be taught on the job. While certification generally is not required, it can be helpful for career advancement. The National Institute for Certification in Engineering Technologies (NICET) is one agency that offers certification programs.

FUTURE PROSPECTS

Engineers are hired by local, state, and federal government agencies as well as by engineering and architectural firms. The Bureau of Labor Statistics (BLS) expects the growth rate for this type of technician career to be on a par with occupational growth generally.

FOR MORE INFORMATION

BOOKS

Brenner, Brian. *Don't Throw This Away! The Civil Engineering Life.* Reston, VA: American Society of Civil Engineers, 2006.

Brenner discusses the practice and mindset of a twenty-first-century engineer.

Sneed, Dani. *Ferris Wheel! George Ferris and His Amazing Invention* (Genius at Work! Great Inventor Biographies). Berkeley Heights, NJ: Enslow Elementary, 2008.

This book explains the ingenuity of George Ferris, whose wheel was a sensation at the 1893 World's Fair.

ORGANIZATIONS

American Society of Civil Engineers
1801 Alexander Bell Drive
Reston, VA 20191-4400
(703) 295-6300, (800) 548-2723
Web site: http://asce.org

This professional society strives to advance engineering technology, encourage lifelong learning, promote the profession, and advocate for environmental stewardship.

Bureau of Labor Statistics (BLS)
Division of Information and Marketing Services
2 Massachusetts Avenue NE, Room 2850
Washington, DC 20212
(202) 691-5200
Web site: http://www.bls.gov
An agency within the U.S. Department of Labor, the BLS measures labor market activity, working conditions, and other economic factors concerning the U.S. labor market. Its *Occupational Outlook Handbook* provides career information on hundreds of occupations. (See http://www.bls.gov/ooh/architecture-and-engineering/civil-engineering-technicians.htm.)

Construction Management Association of America
7926 Jones Branch Drive, Suite 800
McLean, VA 22102-3303
(703) 356-2622
Web site: http://cmaanet.org
The Construction Management Association of America provides numerous construction management resources, including career information for students.

National Institute for Certification in Engineering
  Technologies
1420 King Street
Alexandria, VA 22314-2794
(888) 476-4238
Web site: http://www.nicet.org
The National Institute for Certification in Engineering Technologies provides information about jobs,
  training, and testing for certification.

VIDEOS, BLOGS, AND APPS

"100 Awesome Engineering Projects for Kids."
  Construction Management Degree (http://
  constructionmanagementdegree.org/blog/2010/
  100-awesome-engineering-projects-for-kids).
Simple and fun but instructive projects that demonstrate engineering principals are included on this
  informative blog.

Civil Calculator (FitzgeraldEngineering)
This app provides a collection of civil engineering
  calculations.

Civil Engineering (RangerApps).
This app accesses civil engineering news.

"Eighth Grade Engineering Project Tests Students' Structural Designs." YouTube upload, January 28, 2011 (http://www.youtube.com/watch?v=cMhEootoGyw). Middle school science students have their spaghetti -and-marshmallow building designs tested with a simulated earthquake in this video.

WEB SITES

Due to the changing nature of Internet links, Rosen Publishing has developed an online list of Web sites related to the subject of this book. This site is updated regularly. Please use this link to access the list:

http://www.rosenlinks.com/CCWC/Scien

CHAPTER 2

CAREERS IN AGRICULTURE AND FOOD SCIENCE

When people think of agriculture, they often think of sweaty, dusty farm life. They envision dawn-to-dark toil, with farmers planting, cultivating, and harvesting thousands of acres of corn. Worse, they call to mind disturbing images of corporate operations where poultry, beef, and swine are raised and slaughtered in brutal conditions. If you're toying with the idea of a math or science career, a farm might be the last place you'd expect to work.

However, science and math specialists are crucial for successful food production. To keep food costs down for consumers, scientists strive to find ways to produce food as cheaply and safely as possible. They work to help farmers and food companies grow and market more food and healthier food.

They have a greater concern. Food shortages around the world cause crisis after crisis. Some economists, politicians, historians, and other observers believe the inadequate food supply is the world's most serious problem.

Technology may be the key to better food production. Agricultural and food science technicians help grow, process, preserve, transport, and distribute food more cheaply and efficiently. They work in all areas of food production and with all types of food: grains, vegetables, fruits, and animals.

At the same time, agriculture produces the raw materials for many different consumer products, from clothing to vitamins to livestock and pet feed. Young employees could find agriculture-related jobs in, for example, the textile industry.

Technical jobs are available for science and math enthusiasts who hold no college degree. Technicians work under the supervision of agricultural and food scientists. Some technicians work in the field. Others work in labs.

A scientist applies a pesticide to a potted plant. Technicians help scientists and agricultural workers produce, process, and distribute food economically and safely for consumers.

BIOTECHNOLOGY: AN ANSWER OR AN EVIL?

Some fields of science may lead you into controversial work. Biotechnology, for example, is defined in *Merriam-Webster's Collegiate Dictionary* as "the manipulation…of living organisms or their components" for producing consumer products. With biotechnology, scientists have developed useful medications to fight diseases. They've produced pest-resistant farm crops. Biotechnology has been used for centuries in making cheese and beer and producing many other items, such as biodegradable plastics.

Today, biotechnology has progressed into areas of science that alarm many people. Food scientists are genetically engineering

This chicken is one of millions that have been genetically engineered. Biotechnology has helped produce breeds of poultry that mature faster and are more disease-resistant.

farm animals in an effort to produce more food more affordably. They can produce food faster by manipulating or "redesigning" its makeup (genetics). As a result, we're now raising "identical" chickens by the thousand—each born on the same day and maturing for slaughter on the same day, seven weeks later. Industrial farms are producing more poultry, beef, and pork faster.

This type of production relieves consumer food prices in the United States and, food economists hope, can help feed the hungry in underdeveloped countries. But critics of the system protest filthy, stifling chicken house and stockyard conditions. They also challenge the nutritional value of foods produced this way.

Agricultural field technicians are assigned a wide range of tasks. Here are a few:

- Testing pesticides and herbicides—measuring their effectiveness for pest control as well as assessing possible dangers to humans and animals
- Studying soil erosion—locating the source and proposing solutions
- Planting trees and grasses and helping revitalize exhausted crop soil
- Testing the chemical content of groundwater
- Conducting crop surveys—determining, for example, which seeds fare best in certain soil conditions
- Answering farmers' questions; if they don't have sure answers, they relay the questions to their superiors
- Assisting scientists in the study of breeding techniques

Inside agricultural labs, technical assistants help scientists conduct experiments and record the results. For most assignments in the field or lab, agricultural technicians must keep careful records.

Some agricultural technicians who have a flair for communicating can take to the road. They find employment with companies that make farm implements, fertilizers, and other products that farmers need. Their role is not necessarily to make sales but to demonstrate the products.

PREPARING YOURSELF

Students with an interest in agricultural and food science should learn as much as they can in high school biology, chemistry, and mathematics classes. Some employers require no schooling beyond high school; they train new employees on the job. Others favor applicants who have taken technical school or online courses in life sciences, chemistry, or animal husbandry.

FUTURE PROSPECTS

During the decade 2010 to 2020, the hiring of agricultural and food science technicians is expected to grow by 7 percent, according to the Bureau of Labor Statistics. Technicians work in government offices and laboratories and in corporate labs and processing plants.

FOR MORE INFORMATION

BOOKS

Andrews, Brad. *How to Land a Top-Paying Agricultural and Food Scientist Job: Your Complete Guide to Opportunities, Resumes and Cover Letters, Interviews, Salaries.* Newstead, QLD, Australia: Emereo Pty Ltd., 2011.
This volume provides information on how to apply for a first job in agricultural and food science.

Echaore-McDavid, Susan, and Richard A. McDavid. *Career Opportunities in Agriculture, Food, and Natural Resources.* New York, NY: Checkmark Books, 2010.
This book contains information on more than eighty jobs in agribusiness, forestry, and related areas.

Gladwell, Stephen. *Agricultural & Food Scientists: Job Hunting—A Practical Manual for Job-Hunters and Career Changers.* Newstead, QLD, Australia: Emereo Pty Ltd., 2011.
This book provides advice and strategies for obtaining interviews and finding a job.

Johanson, Paula. *Jobs in Sustainable Agriculture* (Green Careers). New York, NY: Rosen Publishing Group, 2010.

Johanson discusses work on farms as well as related career areas.

ORGANIZATIONS

Agricultural and Applied Economics Association
555 East Wells Street, Suite 1100
Milwaukee, WI 53202
(414) 918-3190
Web site: http://www.aaea.org
The Agricultural and Applied Economics Association is a not-for-profit association for professionals in agriculture and related fields of applied economics.

Bureau of Labor Statistics (BLS)
Division of Information and Marketing Services
2 Massachusetts Avenue NE, Room 2850
Washington, DC 20212
(202) 691-5200
Web site: http://www.bls.gov
An agency within the U.S. Department of Labor, the BLS measures labor market activity, working conditions, and other economic factors concerning the U.S. labor market. Its *Occupational Outlook Handbook* provides career information on hundreds of occupations. (See http://www.bls.gov/ooh/life-physical-and-social-science/agricultural-and-food-science-technicians.htm.)

Council for Agricultural Science and Technology
4420 West Lincoln Way
Ames, IA 50014-3447
(515) 292-2125
Web site: http://www.cast-science.org
The Council for Agricultural Science and Technology
is "the science source for food, agricultural, and
environmental issues."

Institute of Food Technologists
525 West Van Buren, Suite 1000
Chicago, IL 60607
(312) 782-8424
Web site: http://www.ift.org
The Institute of Food Technologists is a "global forum" in
which food technologists from more than one hundred
countries share knowledge and ideas.

U.S. Department of Agriculture
1400 Independence Avenue SW
Washington, DC 20250
(202) 720-2791
Web site: http://www.usda.gov
This federal department oversees all agricultural issues,
including food production, water and forestry issues,
conservation, research, technology, and more.

PERIODICALS

Choices
555 East Wells Street, Suite 1100
Milwaukee, WI 53202
(414) 918-3190
Web site: http://www.choicesmagazine.org/choices
    -magazine
Articles discuss food, farm, and resource issues.

Journal of Food Science
525 West Van Buren, Suite 1000
Chicago, IL 60607
(312) 782-8424
Web site: http://www.ift.org/Knowledge-Center/
    Read-IFT-Publications/Journal-of-Food-Science.aspx
Research papers and reviews cover all aspects of food
    science.

WEB SITES

Due to the changing nature of Internet links, Rosen
Publishing has developed an online list of Web sites
related to the subject of this book. This site is updated
regularly. Please use this link to access the list:

http://www.rosenlinks.com/CCWC/Scien

CHAPTER 3

DENTAL LABORATORY TECHNICIANS

Do you have an interest in art as well as science? Are you intrigued by sculpture, for example? If so, career opportunities are available that let you make use of both skills. One to consider is that of dental lab technician.

These technicians rarely work directly with patients, but they serve patients in very important ways. They contribute not only to dental health but also to the patient's self-esteem. Essentially, they provide a "new mouth" for patients with tooth problems.

Lab technicians create full or partial dentures, bridges, crowns, and other prosthetics (called "dental appliances" in the profession). They work from molds that the dentist makes inside the patient's mouth. With porcelain and metal, the technician can create an exact replica of a tooth or set of teeth.

Steps in the process include:

- Mixing pastes to fill the mold taken by the dentist
- Covering the mold with special mixtures, then letting them firm
- Mounting the prosthetic on a device that simulates the patient's jaw motion and bite

- Carefully studying the shapes and sizes of the teeth and the gaps between
- Sculpting each tooth and other parts of the prosthetic
- Making adjustments to improve the patient's mouth function and make the appliance look natural

Every patient's set of teeth is unique, which makes the restoration process a true art form. Technicians also repair dentures, crowns, and other items that become cracked.

Depending on the patient's needs, dental lab technicians work with ceramics, waxes, metals, plastics, and other materials. Their tools include files, polishers, and small precision instruments, as well as complex machines.

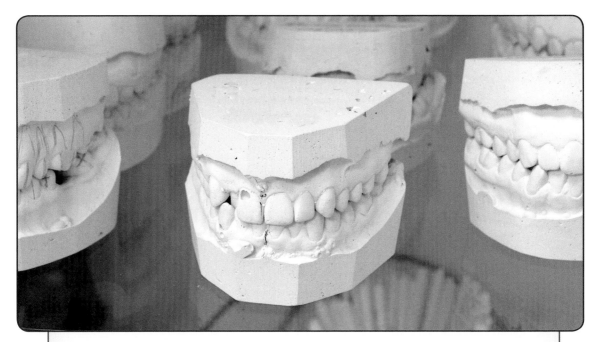

These denture models represent one stage in the work of dental lab technicians. Lab techs construct dentures, bridges, and other prosthetics to precisely fit each patient's mouth.

For some tasks, they wear protective goggles, facemasks, and gloves.

Technicians must have excellent vision because they need to reproduce teeth with just the right shape and color. They must have good eye-hand coordination and finger dexterity. They obviously have to be creative types, and they need the patience of the artist who settles for nothing less than perfection.

Typically, these dental professionals are employed by commercial laboratories. They may also find jobs in dentists' offices and hospitals.

Some labs specialize in one type of restoration; others offer complete services. A technician at a large laboratory may be assigned a specialty task, such as waxing, or may work on just one type of prosthetic. At small labs, a technician usually performs each stage of the restoration process.

When first hired, new technicians mainly work as helpers, pouring the plaster into a mold, for example. As they learn advanced skills, they are given their own assignments. The length of on-the-job training required varies, depending on how the lab operates. Experienced technicians work independently, requiring no supervision.

Some technicians eventually become supervisors in large laboratories, or open labs of their own. Others obtain teaching positions in dental schools or technical schools, as well as hospitals and private companies. Technicians can later find jobs in prosthetic sales and research.

DENTAL TECHNICIAN SPECIALISTS

Some experienced dental lab technicians choose to specialize. They can become certified in any of six areas of specialty: complete dentures, partial dentures, crowns and bridges, orthodontic appliances, ceramics, and implants. Technicians who specialize in making veneers, bridges, and other porcelain and acrylic restorations are dental ceramists.

A lab technician applies porcelain to a mold. Technicians learn to work with a wide variety of precision tools and materials, including porcelains, metals, waxes, and plastics.

Jason J. Kim, a dental ceramist in New York, has become known as a ceramist for Manhattan's rich and famous. The Jason J. Kim Oral Design New York Center (www.jasonjkim.com) collaborates with some of the city's most prominent dentists. Kim promotes "dental aesthetics." He believes each case of dental restoration should be treated as an "individual work of art, creating the perfect, natural smile."

Kim is a coauthor of *Aesthetic Restorative Dentistry: Principles and Practice*. He is also the author of *The Master Ceramist*. He has lectured and taught extensively on the topic.

Technicians who have at least five years of experience can take examinations to qualify as a Certified Dental Technician (CDT).

PREPARING YOURSELF

Courses are available at vocational schools and colleges. Most dental lab technicians, though, learn their skills on the job. Besides applying yourself to science and math studies, it can be useful to take art courses while in high school. Computer skills will be helpful in this profession, too.

FUTURE PROSPECTS

The demand for dental laboratory technicians in coming years is expected to remain steady. However, the demand for these restorations will remain strong. Besides necessary repairs, there is an increasing demand for cosmetic dentistry.

FOR MORE INFORMATION

BOOKS

Boyd, Linda Bartolomucci. *Dental Instruments: A Pocket Guide.* 4th ed. Philadelphia, PA: Saunders (Elsevier), 2011.
This volume includes illustrations and descriptions of more than three hundred dental instruments.
Dofka, Charline M. *Dental Terminology.* 3rd ed. Clifton Park, NY: Delmar Cengage Learning, 2012.
Chapters in this dental "word bank" are organized by specialty area.

ORGANIZATIONS

American Dental Association
211 East Chicago Avenue
Chicago, IL 60611-2678
(312) 440-2500
Web site: http://www.ada.org
The world's largest and oldest national dental society provides oral health information for dentists and patients.

Bureau of Labor Statistics (BLS)
Division of Information and Marketing Services
2 Massachusetts Avenue NE, Room 2850

Washington, DC 20212

(202) 691-5200

Web site: http://www.bls.gov

An agency within the U.S. Department of Labor, the BLS measures labor market activity, working conditions, and other economic factors concerning the U.S. labor market. Its *Occupational Outlook Handbook* provides career information on hundreds of occupations. (See http://www.bls.gov/ooh/production/dental-laboratory-technicians.htm.)

National Association of Dental Laboratories

325 John Knox Road, #L103

Tallahassee, FL 32303

(800) 950-1150

Web site: http://nadl.org

This association advances the dental laboratory technology industry through education, standards, advocacy, and services.

National Board for Certification in Dental Laboratory Technology

325 John Knox Road, #L103

Tallahassee, FL 32303

(800) 684-5310

Web site: http://nbccert.org

The National Board for Certification in Dental Laboratory Technology is the panel that examines candidates for the title of Certified Dental Technician (CDT).

VIDEOS

"A Day-in-the-Life of a Dental Laboratory Technician." YouTube upload, December 22, 2010 (http://www .youtube.com/watch?v=KrT6xNhpzUc).
A dental ceramist takes the viewer through a typical workday, providing detailed photos of her work.

"Dental Laboratory Technician Jobs." YouTube upload, January 29, 2012 (http://www.youtube.com/watch ?v=JrA_9dvlfP0).
This short video shows technicians crafting dentures.

WEB SITES

Due to the changing nature of Internet links, Rosen Publishing has developed an online list of Web sites related to the subject of this book. This site is updated regularly. Please use this link to access the list:

http://www.rosenlinks.com/CCWC/Scien

CHAPTER 4

ELECTRICAL AND ELECTRONICS INSTALLERS AND REPAIRERS

Do you enjoy tinkering with wires and connections? Do you stay with a task until you have everything hooked up correctly? That combination of curiosity, determination, patience, and the desire to make things work marks the mind of an electrical/electronics installer and service technician.

Electrical and electronics installers and repairers perform tasks such as these:

- Installing, troubleshooting, repairing, and replacing motors, gaskets, fuses, and many other parts; to do this, they refer to manuals, schematics, service guides, and manufacturer specifications
- Reassembling and testing repaired equipment
- Keeping records of labor time, parts, and charges
- Providing clients with cost estimates

Electrical equipment virtually surrounds us. Small electrical appliances range from toasters to hair dryers. Major appliances include dishwashers, clothes dryers, and heating and cooling equipment. In industries and institutions, some electrical

Circuit boards, chips, and wafers appear confusing and meaningless to the untrained eye, but electrical and electronics technicians understand them well. They can quickly locate and repair problems.

products are enormous, and installations and repairs are difficult undertakings.

Electronics use power that comes from tiny electrical particles called electrons. Electrons run in circuits, beginning and ending at the same point. When many circuits are put together on the same chip or wafer, they are call integrated circuits. This technology has eliminated the need for wiring and allowed for miniaturization, which means the radio console that took up a corner of the living room fifty years ago can now fit in your pocket.

Circuits operated by microprocessors opened the world to telecommunications. Electronic telecommunications now can connect us to everyone on the planet. Telecommunications equipment includes telephones, radios, fax machines, scanners, garage door openers, alarms, computers, televisions, VCRs, DVD players, video cameras, surround-sound systems, and high-tech weaponry.

Trained workers install and repair these and many other kinds of appliances and equipment. They work in the fields of industry, transportation, utilities, and telecommunications. In industry and business, they deal with electronics such as transmitters, antennas, and control systems. Powerhouse electricians install and maintain electrical systems at powerhouses and substations. In the transportation realm, technicians install and repair navigation, sound, surveillance, and other electronic systems. Specialists handle electrical issues in motor vehicles. Some professionals specialize in fixing electric motors and power tools.

There are two places to perform repairs and testing. Bench technicians work on malfunctioning items brought to their labs or shops. Field technicians take tool kits to the site of the problem (home, office, factory) to work on large machines that cannot easily be transported. Some workers are employed by industries.

Electronic systems are complex. In many situations, repair workers use computer software to test systems and pinpoint problems. They use devices such as multimeters, which measure current, voltage, and other factors. Tools also include signal generators and oscilloscopes, which test and display electronic signals.

While work inside a shop or lab takes place in a clean, controlled environment, work on-site in factories can be

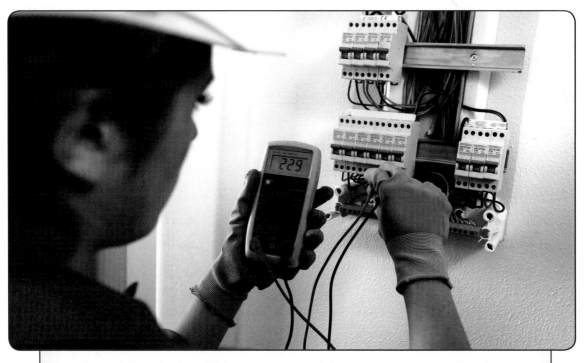

An electrician uses a handheld meter to check each component in a fuse box. Professionals are trained to use various testing and current-measuring devices, as well as computer programs.

dirty, hot, and noisy. This type of work is also hazardous. The Bureau of Labor Statistics reports: "Electric motor, power tools, and related repairers and electrical and electronics installers and repairers of transportation equipment have a higher rate of work-related injuries and illnesses than the average for all other occupations."

Technicians often work from awkward postures. Lifting may be required. They must understand safety procedures and, where necessary, wear hardhats and goggles. If working at heights, they wear harnesses.

Job seekers interested in this line of work naturally must be familiar with electrical equipment and be curious to learn more. They need good vision because they will frequently work with tiny parts and color-coded wiring. Those who work in the field, especially, need good communication skills in order to understand the problems of customers and to explain their solutions.

A SECURE, REWARDING CAREER PATH

Jerry Van Liew has been a hospital electrician in Charleston, South Carolina, for more than thirty years and has found it to be a very rewarding career. "The satisfaction for me is knowing everything in our facility is working, and our patients and staff are happy."

The work requires constant alertness. "The thing I don't like," he says, "is working on live electrical circuits, which can be hazardous if you are not a trained, qualified electrician."

Still, he recommends this type of career for any young person who has a mind for solving problems. By making sure that electrical systems are reliable and safe, these workers perform a tremendous service to society.

It's a secure career path. Van Liew notes, "There will always be a need for electricians."

PREPARING YOURSELF

A college degree isn't necessary to become an installer and repairer. Most job applicants, though, have taken courses at technical schools, community colleges, or online, or they acquired skills while serving in the armed forces. Some equipment makers and software developers also provide training. Apprenticeships are available.

New employees work with and learn from experienced technicians. For career advancement, workers will want to study and obtain certification. Certification exams are given by different organizations, including the Electronics Technicians Association International and the International Society of Certified Electronics Technicians.

FUTURE PROSPECTS

Growth in this job market is continuing, though not as rapidly as in most career fields. The industry will always need new electrical and electronics workers to replace those who retire and transfer to related occupations. Jobs in power-houses, substations, and relay systems will show the most lively growth, along with jobs in electric motor and power tool repair. Labor analysts expect to see little or no growth in commercial, industrial, and transportation equipment installation and repair.

FOR MORE INFORMATION

BOOKS

Gibilisco, Stan. *Teach Yourself Electricity and Electronics.* 4th ed. New York, NY: McGraw-Hill, 2006.
This volume serves as a guide for readers interested in teaching themselves both the basics of electricity and electronics as well as advanced applications, and it offers tips on preparing for licensing exams.

Goetsch, David L. *The Successful Electronics Technician.* Clifton Park, NY: Delmar Cengage Learning, 2007.
This book discusses what it takes to become a successful electronics technician in addition to skills and education.

Traister, John E., and C. Dale Brickner. *Electrician's Exam Preparation Guide to the 2011 NEC.* Carlsbad, CA: Craftsman Book Company, 2011.
This volume prepares students for the National Electrical Code (NEC) exam.

ORGANIZATIONS

Bureau of Labor Statistics (BLS)
Division of Information and Marketing Services
2 Massachusetts Avenue NE, Room 2850

Washington, DC 20212

(202) 691-5200

Web site: http://www.bls.gov

An agency within the U.S. Department of Labor, the BLS measures labor market activity, working conditions, and other economic factors concerning the U.S. labor market. Its *Occupational Outlook Handbook* provides career information on hundreds of occupations. (See http://www.bls.gov/ooh/installation-maintenance-and-repair/electrical-and-electronics-installers-and-repairers.htm.)

Electronics Technicians Association International

5 Depot Street

Greencastle, IN 46135

(800) 288-3824

Web site: http://www.eta-i.org

The Electronics Technicians Association International is a nonprofit, international organization that offers more than fifty certification programs in electronics specialties.

International Society of Certified Electronics Technicians

3608 Pershing Avenue

Fort Worth, TX 76107-4527

(817) 921-9101

Web site: http://www.iscet.org

The International Society of Certified Electronics Technicians offers certification credentials for different competence levels.

National Electrical Contractors Association
3 Bethesda Metro Center, Suite 1100
Bethesda, MD 20814
(301) 657-3110
Web site: http://www.necanet.org
The National Electrical Contractors Association provides news and information for the electrical construction industry.

PERIODICALS

Electrical Contractor
3 Bethesda Metro Center, Suite 1100
Bethesda, MD 20814-5372
(301) 657-3110
Web site: http://www.ecmag.com
This is the official publication of the National Electrical Contractors Association.

Everyday Practical Electronics
Wimborne Publishing Ltd.

113 Lynwood Drive
Merley, Wimborne
Dorset BH21 1UU
United Kingdom
+44 1202 880299
Web site: http://www.epemag3.com
This magazine for electronics hobbyists is published in
    the United Kingdom.

WEB SITES

Due to the changing nature of Internet links, Rosen
Publishing has developed an online list of Web sites
related to the subject of this book. This site is updated
regularly. Please use this link to access the list:

http://www.rosenlinks.com/CCWC/Scien

CHAPTER 5

ENSURING QUALITY

A lot of people are hard to please. Some are picky for no good reason—just to assert dominance and control. Others have very good reasons. They believe we can have a better world if we produce things the right way. They do not crave power, but they insist on top quality. If you think that way, you might make an excellent quality control inspector.

Everything sold in malls, supermarkets, discount centers, and specialty shops underwent a quality inspection before it left the manufacturing plant. Products must meet government standards for safety and durability. Food shouldn't make you sick, gadgets should work in the way they're advertised, and clothes shouldn't rip the first time you put them on. If a product is defective, the results might be highly publicized. No manufacturer wants bad publicity or lawsuits.

Quality control inspectors hired by manufacturers make the "go" or "no go" decision. Duties of quality control inspectors include:

- Studying manufacturing blueprints and specifications

- Observing whether manufacturing processes meet production standards; suggesting changes in the assembly process, if necessary
- Inspecting and testing finished products; this may include making measurements with rulers, calipers, micrometers, and other instruments
- Accepting or rejecting finished products and removing those that don't pass inspection
- Discussing products and production processes with manufacturing supervisors
- Filing reports of their inspection findings and related data

An engineer makes notes while inspecting machinery in a factory. Quality control inspectors perform a great service to society by citing weaknesses and problems, some of which may be dangerous.

Quality control inspectors ensure standards of quality for practically everything that's made and sold. That includes personal and household products such as food, clothes, kitchenware, computers, and smartphones. It includes larger purchases such as cars and prefabricated carports. And it includes industrial items—structural steel, for example.

Some testing procedures are simple, others complex. An inspector may need only the senses—sight, smell, hearing, feel, and taste—to detect a product flaw. More often, an inspector will use measuring tools and electrical, mechanical, and chemical testing devices. Sophisticated diagnostic tools are usually needed.

Inspectors don't rely on their personal feelings and judgments about a product. They use clearly defined test methods to determine if products meet company and government standards.

After inspecting and testing, workers record and report their results. They discuss with manufacturing supervisors possible solutions to any problems they've found.

Some inspectors specialize. Materials inspectors look for scratches, cuts, missing pieces, and other imperfections by examining items by feel, sight, or sound. Mechanical inspectors test to make sure that parts of an item move and fit together correctly; their investigations may probe into electrical and other components of the product.

CONSUMERS AS PRODUCT INSPECTORS

If quality control inspectors don't find the flaws in products before they go on the market, consumer watchdog organizations will blow the whistle soon enough. Effective inspectors, by performing the critical work beforehand, can produce happier buyers. At the same time, they can save manufacturers' reputations.

Consumer Reports (www.consumerreports.org) is a magazine long respected for its no-holds-barred evaluations of products and services. Its mission is "to work for a fair, just, and safe marketplace for all consumers and to empower consumers to protect themselves." Since its founding in 1936, it has helped buyers "distinguish hype from fact and good products from bad ones." In any given issue of the monthly magazine, readers find product comparisons, lab test results, and detailed product information. The comparison findings come from consumers themselves.

Items under study range from food to automobiles to tablet computers to gas grills to health services. One of the magazine's tactics is to have hundreds of "mystery shoppers" and tech experts buy various products from brick-and-mortar stores and online retailers. These consumer representatives test and evaluate the items. Some products get glowing reviews and end up with "*CR* Best Buy" or "Recommended" ratings in the comparisons. Others slip to the bottom of the charts.

Wise manufacturers hire good inspectors to sniff out potential problems before their products come under the scrutiny of market critics.

Math and computer skills are important. Young people interested in this career need an eye for detail and patience for thorough testing. They must have adequate dexterity to remove and examine small product parts. For some assignments, they will be standing for long periods.

Above all, they must have the desire to make sure that things are done right.

PREPARING YOURSELF

A high school diploma is ample for basic product testing. Training is provided on the job. Experienced professionals, however, are needed for jobs that require precision inspecting.

Students can prepare by studying computer-aided design

A mechanical technician makes a careful measurement at a milling machine center. Workers report the findings of their tests and discuss possible solutions if they discover problems.

(CAD) and focusing on science and math classes. Once they're on the job, inspectors can improve career advancement prospects by obtaining a certification from the American Society for Quality.

FUTURE PROSPECTS

Many manufacturers have implemented pretesting and control programs into their production processes. Fewer flaws in the initial stages means the time required for quality control inspection can be reduced.

In spite of those advances, the job market for quality control inspectors is projected to grow at a moderate pace in the near future. Inspectors with advanced skills will be most in demand.

FOR MORE INFORMATION

BOOKS

Webber, Larry, and Michael Wallace. *Quality Control for Dummies*. Hoboken, NJ: Wiley & Sons, Inc., 2012. This volume explains how companies can institute quality control processes.

ORGANIZATIONS

American Society for Quality
611 E. Wisconsin Avenue
P.O. Box 3005
Milwaukee WI 53201-3005
(800) 248-1946
Web site: http://www.asq.org
The American Society for Quality offers certification in different aspects of quality control.

ASTM International
P.O. Box C700
West Conshohocken, PA 19428-2959
(610) 832-9555
Web site: http://www.astm.org

This organization sets technical standards for industries worldwide. The objective is to improve products, enhance safety, facilitate trade, and build consumer confidence.

Bureau of Labor Statistics (BLS)
Division of Information and Marketing Services
2 Massachusetts Avenue NE, Room 2850
Washington, DC 20212
(202) 691-5200
Web site: http://www.bls.gov
An agency within the U.S. Department of Labor, the BLS measures labor market activity, working conditions, and other economic factors concerning the U.S. labor market. Its *Occupational Outlook Handbook* provides career information on hundreds of occupations. (See http://www.bls.gov/ooh/production/quality-control-inspectors.htm.)

Consumer Federation of America
1620 I Street NW, Suite 200
Washington, DC 20006
(202) 387-6121
Web site: http://www.consumerfed.org
This research, education, advocacy, and service organization strives to advance consumer interests.

PERIODICALS

Consumer Reports
101 Truman Avenue
Yonkers, NY 10703-1057
(800) 666-5261
Web site: http://www.consumerreports.org
This watchdog magazine rates products in multiple
    categories, based on consumer input.

WEB SITES

Due to the changing nature of Internet links, Rosen
Publishing has developed an online list of Web sites
related to the subject of this book. This site is updated
regularly. Please use this link to access the list:

http://www.rosenlinks.com/CCWC/Scien

CHAPTER 6

FIBER OPTICS INSTALLERS AND REPAIRERS

Until the late 1900s, most telecommunication networks were connected with copper wiring. Today, most landline phone systems, Internet cable connections, and computer networks use fiber optics instead.

Fiber optics is the transmittal of voices and data, including electronic images, by light pulses (optics) through cables of hairlike, flexible, transparent glass fibers. The technology provides extremely fast communications, more reliable and secure than copper cables, and less expensive. It is not affected by electromagnetic interference and is difficult for hackers to jam or tap.

The Fiber Optic Association (FOA) reports that more than 90 percent of all long-distance voice circuits now employ fiber optics. It is quickly becoming common in home and office installations. The FOA points out that "commercial systems today carry more phone conversations over a pair of fibers than could be carried over thousands of copper pairs."

Optical fiber has also replaced metal wiring in computers, photocopiers, medical equipment, navigation guidance systems, and military weaponry. It is commonly used in security cameras and other alarm systems. Many industries, including automotive, aviation, and engineering, are finding uses for fiber optics.

Jobs in fiber optics include the installation and repair of telecommunication and electrical power systems. Among the typical duties of telecommunications line installers are:

- Installing, maintaining, and repairing equipment
- Laying fiber-optic lines and other cables underground
- Operating power equipment during the installation and repair of lines, poles, and towers
- Testing and inspecting cables

Duties of electrical power line installers include:

- Installing, maintaining, and repairing the lines
- Stringing lines between poles, buildings, and towers; this may involve climbing poles and towers and operating bucket trucks
- Polishing, testing, and inspecting lines, connectors, and equipment
- Locating defects in transformers, voltage regulators, circuit breakers, switches, and fuses

Some fiber technicians assemble fiber-optic cable harnesses. In designing and installing fiber-optic systems that

A specialist examines a cable end in a computer server room. Fiber optic installation and repair sometimes requires working with high-voltage systems, which can be hazardous.

link buildings and people, technicians determine where cable hookups should be placed. They are expected to document certain tasks that they perform.

Fiber optics technicians may also assist engineers in designing and testing new uses for fiber optics. They set up electrical and electronic experiments that could lead to the development of new applications.

Work with fiber optics can be physically demanding and dangerous. Electronic line workers are in contact with high-voltage cables. They sometimes work at dangerous heights. Naturally, they must be trained in the use of safety equipment. They must have good physical dexterity. They should also be willing to work emergency hours; when storms and disasters cause power outages, they must be prepared to respond quickly.

HOW FAST CAN FIBER OPTICS TRANSMIT DATA?

Scientists are experimenting with fiber optics that can transmit more than 100 terabits of data per second through one thin fiber. A terabit is a trillion bits of data. It's been estimated that at 100 terabits (100 trillion bits), people could download three months of high-definition video in one second.

This mind-boggling advance won't likely be available to home or office computer users for some time. One reason is that typical networks can't handle it. Another is that consumers don't need anywhere near that level of communication speed and power...yet. People increasingly are sharing and streaming more data. In years to come, with more and more television and movie offerings online, fiber optics that fast and even faster may become the norm.

PREPARING YOURSELF

High school graduates interested in fiber optics careers should acquire a good understanding of physics and math. Most employers provide extended on-the-job training. Employees may be required to take courses online or at a technical school or community college. Apprenticeship programs are available in some areas. Military personnel may obtain fiber optics training while serving in the armed forces.

Work in fiber optics is done indoors and out. Here, a plant technician checks a roll of cable as a crew prepares to make an installation.

FUTURE PROSPECTS

Job growth between 2010 and 2020 is expected to average 13 percent for fiber optics installers and repairers, according to the U.S. Bureau of Labor Statistics. Employers include electronic and telecommunication companies and manufacturing firms. With society's increasing reliance on fiber optics, the demand for experienced technicians undoubtedly will be strong for the foreseeable future. As in most other technical careers, workers can expect to learn new skills to perform new tasks.

FOR MORE INFORMATION

BOOKS

Downing, James. *Fiber Optic Communications.* Clifton Park, NY: Delmar Cengage Learning, 2004.
This book is a technical guide to fiber optics cabling and devices.

Duree, Galen C. Jr. *Optics for Dummies.* Hoboken, NJ: John Wiley & Sons, 2011.
Duree explains all aspects of the science of light, including fiber optics cabling.

Gibilisco, Stan. *Optics Demystified.* Columbus, OH: McGraw-Hill Professional, 2009.
The author discusses optic science in detail, including optical data transmission technology.

Woodward, Bill, and Emile B. Husson. *Fiber Optics Installer and Technician.* Hoboken, NJ: John Wiley & Sons, 2005.
This practical guide prepares workers for fiber optics installer and fiber optics technician certification.

ORGANIZATIONS

Bureau of Labor Statistics (BLS)
Division of Information and Marketing Services
2 Massachusetts Avenue NE, Room 2850
Washington, DC 20212
(202) 691-5200
Web site: http://www.bls.gov
An agency within the U.S. Department of Labor, the BLS
measures labor market activity, working conditions, and
other economic factors concerning the U.S. labor market. Its *Occupational Outlook Handbook* provides career
information on hundreds of occupations. (See http://
www.bls.gov/ooh/installation-maintenance-and-repair/
line-installers-and-repairers.htm.)

Fiber Optic Association
1119 S. Mission Road, #355
Fallbrook, CA 92028
(760) 451-3655
Web site: http://www.thefoa.org
The Fiber Optic Association is an international professional
society that develops educational programs, approves
training courses, certifies fiber optics and premises
cabling technicians, participates in the creation of industry standards, and generally promotes fiber optics.

Laser Institute of America
13501 Ingenuity Drive, Suite 128
Orlando, FL 32826
(407) 380-1553, (800) 345-2737
Web site: http://www.laserinstitute.org
This institute is a professional society for fostering laser
    applications and safety for the industrial, medical,
    government, and research communities.

The Optical Society
2010 Massachusetts Avenue NW
Washington, DC 20036
(202) 223-8130
Web site: http://www.osa.org
The Optical Society provides information on the science
    of light. It provides articles, a job board, links to other
    sites, and other resources.

U.S. Telecom Association
607 14th Street NW, Suite 400
Washington, DC 20005
(202) 326-7600
Web site: http://www.ustelecom.org
The U.S. Telecom Association is a trade association that
    represents telecom industry suppliers and service
    providers.

PERIODICALS

Applied Optics
2010 Massachusetts Avenue NW
Washington, DC 20036
(202) 223-8130
Web site: http://www.opticsinfobase.org/ao/home.cfm
Articles discuss research into optics applications.

VIDEOS

"Fiber Optics." YouTube upload, May 6, 2007 (http://
www.youtube.com/watch?v=lII8Mf_faVo).
This video shows how optical fiber is manufactured.

Freudenrich, Craig. "How Fiber Optics Work." How Stuff
Works (http://computer.howstuffworks.com/fiber
-optic.htm).
This explains how optical fibers transmit light.

WEB SITES

Due to the changing nature of Internet links, Rosen
Publishing has developed an online list of Web sites
related to the subject of this book. This site is updated
regularly. Please use this link to access the list:

http://www.rosenlinks.com/CCWC/Scien

CHAPTER 7

HAZMAT PROFESSIONALS

Do you have a passion for protecting and cleaning up the environment? Are you willing not just to talk and write about it but to roll up your sleeves, get dirty, and do what you can physically to eliminate pollution? Would you be willing to join in the cleanup of dangerous, possibly life-threatening pollutants? If so, a career as a hazmat technician may be for you.

Hazardous materials (hazmats) are substances that endanger public safety and health. Hazardous materials can harm the ground, water, and air. They include lead, asbestos, radioactive materials, corrosive acids, PCBs, and hundreds of other chemicals. Hazmat crises may result from toxic spills from a ship, train, or truck accident. They may be more subtle discoveries that manufacturing plants have been releasing toxins over a long period of time, poisoning rivers and soil in the area. Nuclear accidents, or even the release of low levels of radioactivity, present threats of contamination. So does biological waste (viruses and bacteria) from hospitals.

Coping with environmental hazards is obviously stressful and dangerous work. First responders may not be sure where the hazard lies or where it is coming from. Different poisons require different methods of handling. Hazmat responders must employ very careful procedures.

Hazmat technicians are usually called to emergencies on short notice. They are sometimes dispatched to contamination sites some distance away, which means that they may have to work away from home for days at a time. Some disasters require long-term cleanup efforts that may take weeks, months, or years.

Contaminated sites are usually cordoned off and the immediate area is evacuated. Technicians often wear protective gear: coveralls and gloves made of special material, hardhats, and face shields or safety glasses. In some situations, they must wear breathing apparatus. To detoxify a site, they use a wide assortment of tools, from brooms to fire hoses. Many firefighters undergo special training to become hazmat technicians. This is logical because firefighters are often the first responders to reports of hazardous contamination.

Hazmat work involves stopping and containing the contamination. It also requires proper collection, storage, and disposal of the poisonous material. Workers carefully package the toxin and transport it to an approved disposal site. Disposal procedures are prescribed and enforced by the U.S. Environmental Protection Agency (EPA).

The federal Occupational Safety and Health Administration (OSHA) requires workers in these positions to complete forty hours of HAZWOPER (Hazardous Waste Operations

Technicians remove asbestos from a lower deck of an aircraft carrier. Hazmat professionals deal with hundreds of products and substances that pose a threat to people and the environment.

and Emergency Response) training. They are taught how to respond to hazmat crises and how to treat, store, and dispose of such materials, as well as how to decontaminate poisoned sites. They learn the properties of dangerous liquids, gases, and substances and how to use protective clothing and gear. They are trained in monitoring the environment and assessing hazardous situations. After they complete HAZWOPER training, workers must take refresher courses periodically.

The growing world population heightens the dangers of pollution. Especially in cities, different forms of human waste

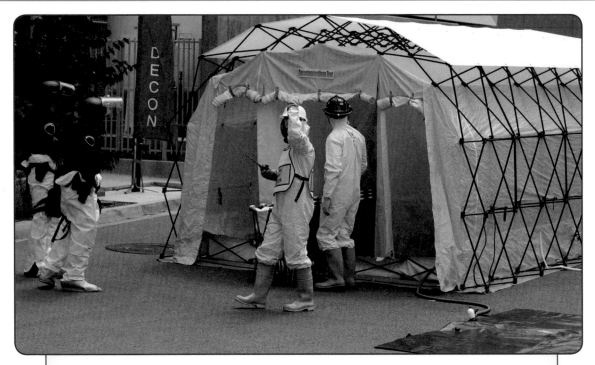

Workers use a portable decontamination shower to ensure they don't touch or breathe harmful chemicals after completing a job. Protective suits, masks, and helmets are vital in their work.

create new environmental hazards. Hazmat technicians play an increasingly important role in keeping the world safe.

PREPARING YOURSELF

A high school diploma is the only educational credential required for many hazmat technician jobs. However, applicants need to have relevant licenses and certificates. The standard credential is the Hazardous Materials Technician certificate, administered by OSHA.

A CLEANUP SUCCESS STORY

Over time, nature it-self can repair damage caused by pollution. Human assistance, though, is needed for faster, more complete healing.

In March 1989, the giant oil tanker *Exxon Valdez* ran aground off the Alaskan coast. An estimated 11 million gallons (41,635,000 liters) of oil spilled into the waters of Prince William Sound. News videos showed wrenching scenes of oil-choked sea animals and the desperate attempts of environmental workers to save them.

During the years of cleanup and legal procedures that followed (the shipping company was ordered to pay millions of dollars for

(Continued on page 70)

Using a high-pressure hose, a worker blasts oil from rock along the shoreline in Prince William Sound in the aftermath of the *Exxon Valdez* oil spill.

(Continued from page 69)

ecological damage), thousands of environmental workers helped the forces of nature reclaim the Alaskan shoreline and restore the region's wildlife to its normal habitat. Although the disaster left an "indelible mark," according to the National Oceanic and Atmospheric Administration (NOAA), the work paid off in bringing the Alaskan shoreline back to life.

Some jobs call for certification as emergency medical technicians (EMTs) and firefighters. Typically, workers are trained in cardiopulmonary resuscitation (CPR) and the use of automated external defibrillators (AEDs). The technician must be a U.S. citizen at least twenty-one years old and must pass a physical exam.

Math skills are important because workers sometimes need to perform mathematical conversions and figure toxicity readings.

FUTURE PROSPECTS

Sadly, career prospects are bright because of constant threats to the environment. Millions of new environmental cleanup jobs have been created since the beginning of the century. Employers include national, state, and local government agencies; private companies that remove hazardous waste; and environmental groups.

FOR MORE INFORMATION

BOOKS

Fanning, Odom. *Opportunities in Environmental Careers.* Rev. ed. New York, NY: McGraw-Hill, 2008.
This volume provides information about various careers, with training and education requirements.

Greenland, Paul R., and Annamarie L. Sheldon. *Career Opportunities in Conservation and the Environment.* New York, NY: Checkmark Books, 2007.
This book includes descriptions of environmental and other outdoor jobs.

Harmon, Daniel E. *Jobs in Environmental Cleanup and Emergency Hazmat Response* (Green Careers). New York, NY: Rosen Publishing, 2010.
Harmon discusses career duties and requirements for workers in earth, air, and water cleanup.

Lewellyn, A. Bronwyn. *Green Jobs: A Guide to Eco-Friendly Employment.* Avon, MA: Adams Media, 2008.
This volume identifies "green-collar" jobs and explains necessary education and training.

Ollhoff, Jim. *Hazmat* (Emergency Workers). Minneapolis, MN: ABDO Publishing, 2012.
Ollhoff describes the types of hazardous materials and how trained technicians handle them.

ORGANIZATIONS

Bureau of Labor Statistics (BLS)
Division of Information and Marketing Services
2 Massachusetts Avenue NE, Room 2850
Washington, DC 20212
(202) 691-5200
Web site: http://www.bls.gov
An agency within the U.S. Department of Labor, the BLS measures labor market activity, working conditions, and other economic factors concerning the U.S. labor market. Its *Occupational Outlook Handbook* provides career information on hundreds of occupations. (See http://www.bls.gov/ooh/construction-and-extraction/hazardous-materials-removal-workers.html.)

Green for All
1611 Telegraph Avenue, Suite 600
Oakland, CA 94612
(510) 663-6500

Web site: http://www.greenforall.org

This is a national organization that seeks to "curb global warming and oil dependence" in an effort to create green jobs, "safer streets, and healthier communities."

Pipeline and Hazardous Materials Safety Administration

U.S. Department of Transportation
East Building, 2nd Floor
1200 New Jersey Avenue SE
Washington, DC 20590
(202) 366-4595
Web site: http://www.phmsa.dot.gov/hazmat

This federal organization works to protect people and the environment from the risks of transporting hazardous materials by pipeline and other modes of transportation.

U.S. Environmental Protection Agency (EPA)
Ariel Rios Building
1200 Pennsylvania Avenue NW
Washington, DC 20460
(202) 272-0167
Web site: http://www.epa.gov

This federal agency is responsible for implementing and enforcing environmental laws.

VIDEOS

"Hazardous Materials Team Training." YouTube upload, July 14, 2009 (http://www.youtube.com/watch ?v=tw7xmCSuV1s).
This video shows firefighters in a hazmat technician training class.

"Responding to Hazmat Incidents." YouTube upload, January 15, 2009 (http://www.youtube.com/watch?v=mpww9z-tXAI).
This video shows emergency workers responding to hazmat calls.

WEB SITES

Due to the changing nature of Internet links, Rosen Publishing has developed an online list of Web sites related to the subject of this book. This site is updated regularly. Please use this link to access the list:

http://www.rosenlinks.com/CCWC/Scien

CHAPTER 8

KEEPING THE WATER CLEAN

Nothing can live without water. Clean water is essential for good health. In towns and cities, keeping water clean is the task of water treatment plant and water systems operators.

After we use it for drinking, cooking, and cleaning, what happens to the wastewater? Returning safe water to the earth, rivers, and oceans is essential for the health of our communities and the whole planet. Much of this responsibility falls to operators of wastewater treatment plants and systems.

Operators can take great pride in their careers overseeing water and wastewater treatment. While performing a fundamental service for society, they take on challenging job roles.

Much is involved in delivering safe, clean water from rivers, lakes, and underground reservoirs to our homes, workplaces, and public facilities. It's also a complicated (and costly) task to transform used water from sewers, drain pipes, and industrial waste facilities into a condition that's safe to return to the earth. Both ways, water flows through a network of pipes. At some point, between the consumer and the earth, it passes through a chemical treatment plant to make it as pure as possible.

Plants run a sophisticated system of machines. With modern technology, the machines are linked. They can be operated and monitored by the plant operator at a control board.

Here are some of the duties of water system operators:

- Operating, inspecting, and maintaining equipment
- Monitoring meters, gauges, and operating conditions
- Regularly collecting and testing samples of water and sewage for parasites, bacteria, and other contaminants
- Making records of data, such as the readings on gauges and meters
- Adding chlorine, ammonia, lime, and other chemicals to disinfect (purify) the water

In major municipalities, wastewater treatment plants are vast facilities that run constantly. Yet, modern systems can be operated and monitored by a small shift crew.

- Cleaning water tanks, filters, and work areas
- Keeping abreast of local and federal environmental regulations
- Making sure that the facility is safe for workers

Treatment plants operate constantly. Thanks to advanced technology, it's possible for one or two workers per shift to run the entire plant in small facilities. Large plants require a team of operators for each shift. On teams, individuals are assigned specialized duties.

The job is not without unpleasant elements. Odors and machine noise are common. Some physical exertion is required, and operators often climb to considerable heights for tank inspections and maintenance. There are hazards such as slippery surfaces and possible emissions of harmful gas.

Operators must respond quickly to emergencies. These can include machine malfunctions, chemical leaks, and crises brought on by nature—flooding, for instance, which can overflow a plant's sewage capacity. Less urgent but pressing needs can cause operators to work overtime.

About three-fourths of plant and system operators work for local government agencies. Others work for private companies that are contracted by towns and cities to treat water and sewage. New hires don't start out as operators; they usually begin as trainees and then become attendants, then operators-in-training. Some large plants provide study programs.

A scientist in a water treatment plant laboratory labels chemical bottles. Workers regularly take water and sewage samples to make sure both citizens and the environment are safe from pollution.

Math, as well as mechanical skills, is important for this career. Operators regularly work with formulas and data to maintain proper water and concentration levels.

PREPARING YOURSELF

A high school diploma or equivalent is sufficient. Agencies that run some of the larger treatment plants prefer job candidates who have associate's degrees in water/wastewater

THE CRITICAL IMPORTANCE OF WATER TREATMENT

In underdeveloped countries, approximately three million early deaths each year are linked to diseases associated with drinking water. According to the Worldometers statistics project (www.worldometers.info/water), some five thousand children in those regions die every day from diarrhea alone.

In the United States, waterborne threats are far less common, thanks largely to the proper treatment of drinking water and wastewater. Even so, reports the National Center for Biotechnology Information (NCBI, http://www.ncbi.nlm.nih.gov/pubmed/18020305), "they do still occur and can lead to serious acute, chronic, or sometimes fatal health consequences." The U.S. Centers for Disease Control and Prevention (CDC) says approximately nine hundred Americans die each year from waterborne infections, and some nine hundred thousand others get sick.

Properly functioning treatment plants, the NCBI concludes, eliminate most of the dangerous bacteria, fungi, and viruses from our water systems. The EPA sets standards to ensure safe drinking water. It works with regional, state, and local agencies to enforce the Safe Water Drinking Act. Among other regulations, the EPA establishes limits on the levels of contaminants allowed in public water systems: "The legal limits reflect both the level that protects human health and the level that water systems can achieve using the best available technology." The EPA also imposes testing schedules and methods for water system operations.

quality management and treatment technology. Operators must have state licenses. In some states, different license levels determine the size of the treatment facility a worker can operate.

FUTURE PROSPECTS

Employment in this job category likely will grow by 12 percent between 2010 and 2020, according the Bureau of Labor Statistics. More treatment plants will be built and existing ones will be expanded as the population increases. New government regulations may call for more advanced treatment systems; this means operators will have to learn more sophisticated systems and controls.

FOR MORE INFORMATION

BOOKS

Fasulo, Mike, and Paul Walker. *Careers in the Environment.* New York, NY: McGraw-Hill, 2007.
Descriptions of environmental careers and tips for finding jobs are included.

Howe, Kerry J., et al. *Principles of Water Treatment.* Hoboken, NJ: Wiley & Sons, Inc., 2012.
This work includes material on treatment plant operation.

Rudman, Jack. *Water Plant Operator* (Career Examination Series). Syosset, NY: National Learning Corporation, 2008.
This book is a test preparation study guide with questions and answers.

ORGANIZATIONS

American Water Works Association
6666 West Quincy Avenue
Denver, CO 80235
(303) 794-7711, (800) 926-7337
Web site: http://www.awwa.org
This association offers educational resources and advocates for safe, sustainable water supplies.

Association of Water Technologies
9707 Key West Avenue, Suite 100
Rockville, MD 20850
(301) 740-1421
Web site: http://www.awt.org
This organization of water treatment companies provides
    training, certification, and awareness programs.

Bureau of Labor Statistics (BLS)
Division of Information and Marketing Services
2 Massachusetts Avenue NE, Room 2850
Washington, DC 20212
(202) 691-5200
Web site: http://www.bls.gov
An agency within the U.S. Department of Labor, the BLS
    measures labor market activity, working conditions, and
    other economic factors concerning the U.S. labor mar-
    ket. Its *Occupational Outlook Handbook* provides career
    information on hundreds of occupations. (See http://
    www.bls.gov/ooh/construction-and-extraction/
    hazardous-materials-removal-workers.htm and http://
    www.bls.gov/ooh/production/water-and-wastewater
    -treatment-plant-and-system-operators.htm.)

U.S. Environmental Protection Agency
Ariel Rios Building

1200 Pennsylvania Avenue NW
Washington, DC 20460
(202) 272-0167
Web site: http://www.epa.gov
The EPA provides extensive information on
    water-related issues.

Water Quality Association
4151 Naperville Road
Lisle, IL 60532-3696
(630) 505-0160
Web site: http://www.wqa.org
This association represents the residential, commercial,
    and industrial water treatment industry and provides
    information and educational sources.

WEB SITES

Due to the changing nature of Internet links, Rosen
Publishing has developed an online list of Web sites
related to the subject of this book. This site is updated
regularly. Please use this link to access the list:

http://www.rosenlinks.com/CCWC/Scien

CHAPTER 9

LENDING MONEY

If you're good at math, you should be good at managing your money. You understand how much needs to come in (income) to pay for what you spend. Hopefully, you're budgeting. After your weekly or monthly allowance or part-time job income is balanced against your expenses during that period, you should be "in the black." That means you'll have earned more than you spent. Ideally, you'll have a little money left to put into a savings account.

If you spend more than you earn during a particular budget period, you're "in the red."

When you become an adult, you'll find that money matters can be very complicated. For example, most people—young and old—who need to buy a car don't have enough money in their savings account to pay for it. They have to borrow money.

Most people need to borrow money to buy a house. They borrow money to buy many other things they need. (All too often, they borrow money to pay for things they don't really need.)

Loan officers are math-minded professionals who work with consumers who want to borrow money. Generally, the process works this way:

- They meet with the loan applicant to obtain information and answer questions about the lending system; they explain the different types of loans available and the terms and conditions of each one.
- They gather the loan applicant's financial information (income, monthly expenses, debts, credit rating, etc.) and verify it.
- After examining the applicant's financial data, they either approve the loan application or refer the case to their superiors.

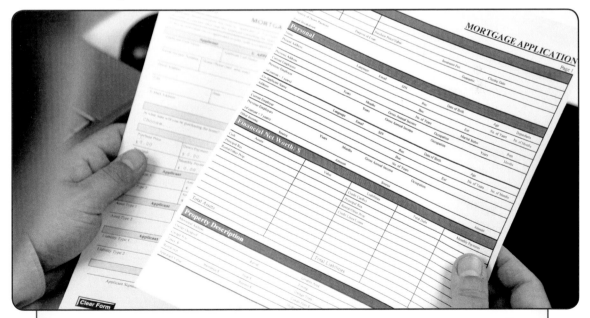

Obtaining a loan may require the completion of much paperwork, especially for mortgage loans. The process begins with a basic mortgage application. Applicants may need to provide detailed financial information.

The key question is whether the loan applicant will be able to pay back the loan, making regular monthly payments on time.

Lending institutions use computer software and formulas to calculate the loan applicant's financial status. Software can make an automated recommendation about the wisdom of making the loan based on numbers. But that may not tell the complete story. Loan officers take into account any related circumstances in the case, then make the lending decision.

There are different types of loan officers. They make different types of loans. Generally, loans fall into one of these categories:

- Commercial loans are loans to businesses that need funds for start-up or expansion. Commercial loans are usually complex and involve large amounts of money. Some require the involvement of two or more banking institutions.
- Consumer loans are loans to individuals or couples. People use these loans for such necessities as buying cars and paying college tuition fees.
- Mortgage loans are for buying homes, office buildings, and other real estate.

Commercial and mortgage loan officers often meet with clients at their homes or places of business. Consumer loan officers typically meet with clients in loan company offices.

Some loan officers work for banks and other lending companies that actively look for new business. They're expected

"SECURED" AND "UNSECURED" LOANS—WHAT'S THE DIFFERENCE?

Loan officers will become intimately familiar with many types of loans. A general distinction is secured versus unsecured loans.

For a secured loan, the borrower offers an asset (called "collateral") to guarantee payback in case the borrower is unable to pay back the money on time. The asset on a car loan may be the car itself; if the borrower fails to make payments, the lender takes the car.

For an unsecured loan, the borrower offers no collateral. That means the loan is more risky for the lender. As a result, the interest rates charged for unsecured loans are much higher than those for secured loans.

to make calls to seek new customers. Sales and marketing skills can be great assets in landing this type of job.

Math skills are important for comparing monetary items. Loan officers also need sound decision-making abilities.

PREPARING YOURSELF

For most loan officer positions, a high school diploma is the only educational requirement. Commercial loan officers, who

Young people sometimes need loans for such purposes as buying a car and covering college expenses. Their parents or guardians may be required to obtain the loan for them.

must have an understanding of business accounting, need a degree in business, finance, economics, or a similar major. Mortgage loan officers must be licensed; licensing requires at least twenty college credit hours. In other scenarios, loan officers learn on the job. Most lending companies have their own training programs.

Certification is usually not required, but it can broaden advancement opportunities. Certification courses are offered by banking associations and colleges. Workers who will be using underwriting software may need to take software classes.

FUTURE PROSPECTS

The lending industry was devastated by the recession of the early 2000s. Economists expect it to rebound. The Bureau of Labor Statistics projects that loan officer employment will grow by 14 percent between 2010 and 2020. But numerous factors affect the borrowing/lending market, such as interest rates and national economic growth. The demand for loans will go up and down as the overall economic picture changes from year to year.

FOR MORE INFORMATION

APPS

FlatBranch Mortgage Calculator (9magnets, LLC)
This is an "intuitive and elegant" app for calculating and
    managing a home mortgage.

Loan Calculator—LoanDroid (StarvingMind)
This loan calculator app features large, touch-type keys for
    fast number entry.

Loan Officer (Murray Hill Technologies)
This simple-to-use app can make loan calculations.

Money Manager (+PC Editing) (Realbyte Co., Ltd.)
This app helps manage information about personal assets.
Mortgage Rates, Credit Card Rates and Mortgage
    Calculators (ERATE.com)
This app provides rates, fees, monthly payments, and
    other mortgage loan information.

SNMC Calculator (Russ Warner)
This app calculates payment and amortizations on new
    loans and refinances. It also calculates how large a

loan an individual might qualify for and provides a request-for-information form.

BOOKS

Gladwell, Stephen. *Loan Officers: Job Hunting— A Practical Manual for Job-Hunters and Career Changers.* Newstead, QLD, Australia: Emereo Pty Ltd., 2011.
Gladwell explains what loan officers do, how they go about their work, and what training is needed.

Mazzola, James O. *Loan Officer Book: Earn Six Figures Without a College Education.* Scotts Valley, CA: CreateSpace Independent Publishing Platform (On-Demand Publishing, LLC), 2011.
This book discusses how loan officers can thrive even "in the wake of the housing bubble bust."

ORGANIZATIONS

American Academy of Financial Management
1670-F E. Cheyenne Mountain Boulevard, Box 293
Colorado Springs, CO 80906
(504) 495-1748
Web site: http://www.aafm.us

This organization provides standards and certification for professionals in the financial sector.

Association for Financial Professionals
4520 East-West Highway, Suite 750
Bethesda, MD 20814
(301) 907-2862
Web site: http://www.afponline.org
The Association for Financial Professionals provides news and information for professionals in the finance sector.

Bureau of Labor Statistics (BLS)
Division of Information and Marketing Services
2 Massachusetts Avenue NE, Room 2850
Washington, DC 20212
(202) 691-5200
Web site: http://www.bls.gov
An agency within the U.S. Department of Labor, the BLS measures labor market activity, working conditions, and other economic factors concerning the U.S. labor market. Its *Occupational Outlook Handbook* provides career information on hundreds of occupations. (See http://www.bls.gov/ooh/business-and-financial/loan-officers.htm.)

National Association of Mortgage Brokers
2701 W. 15th Street, Suite 536
Plano, TX 75075
(972) 758-1151
Web site: http://www.namb.org
This association represents the interests of mortgage
    professionals and buyers, promoting professionalism
    and ethical standards.

WEB SITES

Due to the changing nature of Internet links, Rosen
Publishing has developed an online list of Web sites
related to the subject of this book. This site is updated
regularly. Please use this link to access the list:

http://www.rosenlinks.com/CCWC/Scien

CHAPTER 10

AEROSPACE ENGINEERING AND OPERATIONS TECHNICIANS

The vocational field of aerospace is concerned with vehicles that fly into the skies and probe outer space. Aerospace engineering and operations technicians help engineers design, develop, test, and construct aircraft and spacecraft. These include multimillion-dollar vehicles like helicopters and small airplanes. They also include multi-billion-dollar projects like the International Space Station.

Much of the work is testing. Technicians are engaged in programming and testing new part and product designs with computer simulations. The failure of one small part in flight could result in a major catastrophe. Technicians run computer-testing systems and record test results concerning parts and assembly work. They discuss these findings with the engineers who designed the parts. A technician may work for a year or longer to help perfect one small part.

Technicians help create the parts and systems that will be tested. They install instruments and electronic and mechanical equipment on planes and spacecraft.

An example of aircraft instrumentation is the flight management computer. This instrument shows the craft's altitude, course, and speed, factoring in wind conditions and course information. Another vital tool is the instrument landing system, which helps pilots find their way to an airport runway through darkness and storms. A technology called the microwave landing system can help land a plane electronically, if necessary.

Some aerospace technicians work at a more basic level, helping build test facilities.

Most technicians are employed by manufacturers of aerospace parts and products. Others work for makers of navigation, control, and measuring instruments. A small

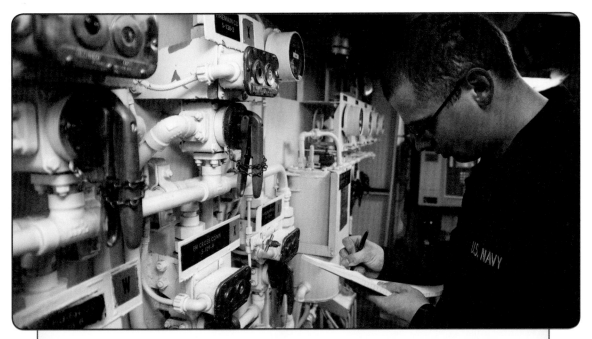

Much work in the aerospace field is done on military projects. Here, a naval damage control fireman inspects power-indicating deck lights aboard an aircraft carrier.

percentage work with firms providing engineering, architectural, and air transportation services.

As the word "technician" suggests, these workers require technical skills. They help build the new technology that aerospace engineers design. Math skills are critical in this line of work. Technicians use math principles in design, analysis, and troubleshooting. They also need to think critically. They help their engineering supervisors

AVIATION TERMS

Aeronautics technology has created a dictionary of its own. Here are just a few of the acronyms (initialized abbreviations) you'll use if you embark in this career field:

- EICAS (Engine-Indicating and Crew-Alerting System). This displays the status of the engine and other features of an aircraft that are important to its safety.
- FADEC (Full-Authority Digital Engine Control). This controls the fuel for an airplane's throttle and the autopilot.
- HUGS (Head-Up Guidance System). This displays information about the aircraft. It is designed so that the pilot can look directly out the window while reading the screen.
- ILS (Instrument Landing System). This aligns the aircraft with the runway on the final approach before landing.
- IRS (Inertial Reference System). This is a laser gyroscope that gives the pilot information about the plane's attitude and acceleration.

identify problems and determine why a product design isn't working correctly.

Other important qualities include attention to detail and good communication skills. Technicians routinely carry out detailed instructions handed down by engineers.

High school students interested in this type of job should focus on math and science classes. Computer-related courses will be especially valuable. So are courses in drafting. Any course that helps develop hand skills is useful because aerospace technicians are, among other things, builders.

Aerospace technicians work full-time in manufacturing plants, labs, and offices. In factories, they help construct airplanes, spacecraft, and military rockets and missiles. Some

The cockpit console of an airplane presents complex panels of controls and displays. Aerospace technicians help engineers create, install, and test aircraft instrument systems.

technicians in this field work on military defense projects. This requires security clearance.

PREPARING YOURSELF

Some vocational school programs offer a diploma and certification to equip a student for a career as an aerospace engineering and operations technician. Many workers in this field go through two-year programs in aerospace technology or related areas of study. They take courses in physics, chemistry, computer science, mechanical drawing, electronics, and other subjects. Employers typically provide training on the job; apprenticeships may be available. High school graduates can obtain valuable training in this line in the armed forces.

Certification is usually not required, but it certainly can help in career advancement. The U.S. Federal Aviation Administration (FAA) offers certification information.

FUTURE PROSPECTS

Jobs in this industry seem secure, although the Bureau of Labor Statistics projects no significant job growth between 2010 and 2020. The BLS observes that technicians working on engines and propulsion systems will be especially in demand. That's because government regulators press for aircraft engines that use less fuel and make less noise.

FOR MORE INFORMATION

BLOGS

Aerospace Blog
http://aerospaceblog.wordpress.com
This blog links to articles published in the aviation and
    aerospace press.

Aviation Week
http://www.aviationweek.com
Aviation Week magazine sponsors blogs on commercial
    and defense aviation, space, and other aeronautical
    developments.

Avjobs.com
http://www.avjobs.com/blog
Up-to-date job openings for various positions in the
    aviation industry are discussed in this blog.

JP Aerospace
http://jpaerospace.com/blog
This is the blog site of JP Aerospace, an independent space
    program with projects developed by volunteers.

NASA
http://blogs.nasa.gov/cm/newui/blog/blogs.jsp

A variety of current and archived blogs are maintained by the National Aeronautics and Space Administration.

The Uptime Blog/Enigma
http://uptimeblog.enigma.com/the-uptime-blog/tabid/50748/Default.aspx?Tag=aviation%20maintenance%20technicians
This blog includes posts about "the challenges and opportunities facing maintenance professionals as they strive to improve product maintenance and support, lower costs, and add revenue via enhanced aftermarket."

ORGANIZATIONS

Aircraft Electronics Association
3570 NE Ralph Powell Road
Lee's Summit, MO 64064
(816) 347-8400
Web site: http://www.aea.net
This association represents aviation businesses, including those specializing in maintenance, repair, and installation of avionics and electronic systems in general aviation aircraft.

Bureau of Labor Statistics (BLS)
Division of Information and Marketing Services

2 Massachusetts Avenue NE, Room 2850
Washington, DC 20212
(202) 691-5200
Web site: http://www.bls.gov
An agency within the U.S. Department of Labor, the
   BLS measures labor market activity, working conditions, and other economic factors concerning the
   U.S. labor market. Its *Occupational Outlook Hand-*
   book provides career information on hundreds of
   occupations. (See http://www.bls.gov/ooh/
   architecture-and-engineering/aerospace
   -engineering-and-operations-technicians.htm.)

National Center for Aerospace & Transportation
   Technologies
P.O. Box 136818
Fort Worth, TX 76136
(817) 984-4738
Web site: http://www.ncatt.org
This center develops national standards and certifications
   for industry professionals.

Professional Aviation Maintenance Association
972 E. Tuttle Road, Building 204
Ionia, MI 48846

(800) 356-1671
Web site: http://www.pama.org
This organization promotes professionalism for aviation
    maintenance technicians through education, skill
    improvement, and information.

U.S. Federal Aviation Administration
800 Independence Avenue SW
Washington, DC 20591
(866) 835-5322
Web site: http://www.faa.gov
Anyone interested in this career field should explore
    the information and resources provided by the U.S.
    Federal Aviation Administration.

WEB SITES

Due to the changing nature of Internet links, Rosen
Publishing has developed an online list of Web sites
related to the subject of this book. This site is updated
regularly. Please use this link to access the list:

http://www.rosenlinks.com/CCWC/Scien

CHAPTER 11

MEDICAL APPLIANCE TECHNICIANS

In years past, the loss or permanent injury of a limb doomed people to lives of dismal dependence. Losses are caused by accidents or by infections that result in amputation. Some result from birth defects, while others occur in the course of the aging process. Previously, these impairments often left victims humiliated and outcast. Physical activities were drastically restricted. Job prospects were meager to nonexistent.

No longer! Advances in medical technology have returned many injured individuals to normal, active lifestyles. They use highly effective attachments, including prosthetic limbs, leg and foot braces, and arch supports. Facial replacement parts can restore a normal appearance after a severe injury or surgery. Hearing aids are comfortably fitted.

The skilled workers who create these devices are medical appliance technicians. This fascinating, highly satisfying career field is open to high school graduates.

Surgical specialists known as prosthetists design and fit body replacement parts. Orthotists are medical scientists who design braces and other supports to relieve pain and

Artificial limbs help amputees live active, happy, and productive lives. Medical appliance technicians construct many kinds of prostheses, carefully following designs developed by surgical specialists.

permit better movement. Podiatrists are doctors who specialize in solving foot problems. The replacement and support devices they design are called medical appliances.

These medical professionals carefully measure and prescribe an appliance to precisely fit patients. They turn the prescriptions (work orders) over to medical appliance technicians to construct the devices. Technicians proceed as follows:

- They study the work order carefully.
- They determine what materials and hand and power tools to use.

A DAWNING AGE OF SUPERHUMANS?

Hugh Herr enjoys rock climbing. Scaling a 200-foot (61-meter) sheer rock face is, for him, both a thrill and a piece of cake. But it's astonishing and a bit unnerving to watch him maneuver upward in one of his rather risky outings. Herr has prosthetic legs.

Herr has always enjoyed mountaineering. As a teenager in 1982, he and a friend were caught in a blizzard while climbing Mount Washington in New Hampshire. They survived by fashioning snow caves until they were rescued. The physical damage to his frozen legs, though, was permanent. Both legs had to be amputated above the knees.

Thanks to prosthetic limbs, Herr is as adventuresome and agile as ever. In a 2012 interview with the *Daily Mail* (London, UK), Herr said he believes modern prosthetics are doing more than simply enabling people with disabilities. He thinks advances in the design and construction of medical appliances can result in artificial limbs that are superior to biological limbs. For example, "amputees will be able to walk with less energy than a person with biological legs," he told the paper.

Herr operates a laboratory at the Massachusetts Institute of Technology where artificial legs are made.

- They lay out and mark dimensions to create a basic pattern for unmolded, unshaped metal and plastic; they then bend, shape, and form the material.
- They polish the appliance.

- After completion, they use meters and other instruments to test the appliance for correct movement and alignment.
- Over time, they may be called on to alter or repair a device, again following the prescription of the health care professional.

Most medical appliance technicians work in manufacturing labs. They use special machinery and tools in working with reconstructive materials. The work requires technical skills to operate the equipment properly. Some projects call for riveting and welding. The job also calls for creative thinking and excellent analytical skills because appliances must be made to fit perfectly. In some settings, technicians work in teams, so they need good interpersonal skills.

Some of the materials they use can be hazardous if not handled properly. Technicians sometimes wear gloves, face-masks, and goggles.

While in high school, students interested in this career should especially focus on math and science classes. They should also take computer classes, as well as wood and metal shop training.

PREPARING YOURSELF

New medical appliance technicians typically learn their skills from experienced professionals on the job, with no need for

An appliance technician completes a molding of a plaster cast that will be used to build an artificial leg. The work calls for skills handling precision tools and machinery.

college courses. The length of training varies, depending on the company's policies and how fast the individual learns. Some technicians train for more than a year before they're assigned to create a medical appliance independently. A few technical and community colleges offer courses helpful for medical appliance construction.

Certification is not required, but it can enhance employment and advancement prospects. The American Board for Certification in Orthotics, Prosthetics and Pedorthics administers certification exams. Some technicians later take advanced education to become prosthetists and orthotists.

FUTURE PROSPECTS

Advances in automation generally mean fewer people can accomplish more work. This is slowing the projected rate of growth for medical appliance technicians to below the job market average. However, the need for technicians remains strong, especially because of an aging population. Older people in particular are affected by cardiovascular ailments and diabetes—the main causes of limb loss. The elderly are also more likely to require foot braces and other support devices.

FOR MORE INFORMATION

BOOKS

Kaster, Pam. *Molly the Pony: A True Story.* Baton Rouge, LA: Louisiana State University Press, 2008.
Kaster tells an inspiring story of prosthetics in veterinary care.

May, Bella, and Margery A. Lockard. *Prosthetics & Orthotics in Clinical Practice.* Philadelphia, PA: F. A. Davis Company, 2011.
The authors present case studies with more than five hundred photographs and illustrations.

ORGANIZATIONS

American Academy of Orthotists and Prosthetists
1331 H Street NW, Suite 501
Washington, DC 20005
(202) 380-3663
Web site: http://www.oandp.org
This academy provides information for advancing patient care standards. It also offers career guidance.

American Board for Certification in Orthotics, Prosthetics and Pedorthics

330 John Carlyle Street, Suite 210
Alexandria, VA 22314
(703) 836-7114
Web site: http://www.abcop.org
This board provides certification for technicians who pass
an examination.

Bureau of Labor Statistics (BLS)
Division of Information and Marketing Services
2 Massachusetts Avenue NE, Room 2850
Washington, DC 20212
(202) 691-5200
Web site: http://www.bls.gov
An agency within the U.S. Department of Labor, the BLS
measures economic factors concerning the U.S. labor
market. Its *Occupational Outlook Handbook* provides
career information on hundreds of occupations. (See
http:// www.bls.gov/ooh/production/medical-appliance
-technicians.htm.)

National Association for the Advancement of
Orthotics and Prosthetics (NAAOP)
1501 M Street NW, 7th Floor
Washington, DC 20005-1700
(202) 624-0064, (800) 622-6740
Web site: http://www.naaop.org

The NAAOP provides help and information to orthotic and prosthetics patients.

VIDEOS AND PODCASTS

Career Cornerstone Center
http://www.careercornerstone.org/medtech/medappltech/medappltech.htm
This audio podcast describes what medical appliance technicians do and how they go about their work.

"The Height of Courage: Climber Scales 200ft Cliff Despite Having No Legs." *Daily Mail*, July 31, 2012. Retrieved March 2013 (http://www.dailymail.co.uk/news/article-2181527/Who-Says-I-Cant-climber-scales-200ft-cliff-despite-having-legs--false-limbs-falling-halfway-up.html).
This online post includes photos and a video of Hugh Herr making a climb with his prosthetic legs.

WEB SITES

Due to the changing nature of Internet links, Rosen Publishing has developed an online list of Web sites related to the subject of this book. This site is updated regularly. Please use this link to access the list:

http://www.rosenlinks.com/CCWC/Scien

CHAPTER 12

OCCUPATIONAL HEALTH AND SAFETY

Safety on the job is the concern of occupational health and safety technicians. They make sure that workplaces conform to government health and safety regulations. By doing so, they help protect workers while helping company owners avoid costly problems.

The duties of occupational health and safety technicians are:

- Visiting workplaces to inspect and test equipment and conditions and to evaluate the way employees work. The objective is to make sure that the work environment meets government safety and health requirements.
- Taking samples of materials that might be poisonous (mold, dust, vapors). Other professionals known as occupational health and safety specialists will examine the samples in a laboratory.
- Working with health and safety specialists, seeking solutions to hazards and potential hazards.
- Conducting and evaluating workplace health and safety programs.

- Demonstrating how to properly use safety equipment and store hazardous materials.

Another role of health and safety technicians is that of detective. They investigate workplace accidents to determine what caused them and how to avoid them in the future.

Almost a fourth of technicians are hired by local and state governments. The others work for many different employers, such as hospitals, mines and quarries, factories, offices, and oil rigs. Some work for consulting services that perform inspections under contract for companies and institutions. About 5 percent are employed by waste management and remediation services.

Some technicians focus on particular categories of workplace safety and health. Environmental protection techs, for example, work with the handling and storage of hazardous waste. They investigate air pollution and sometimes are involved in cleanup projects.

Industrial hygiene technicians look for the threat of contagious diseases. They also seek traces of poisons, including pesticides, lead, and asbestos. Similarly, health physics technicians examine workplaces where radioactive material is used, looking for evidence of dangerous exposure levels.

Mine examiners are concerned mainly with airflow. Improper ventilation can result in a buildup of harmful gases.

Inspectors examine the condition of underground rock walls. Occupational health and safety specialists make sure working conditions meet government standards. They discuss how companies can resolve any problems they find.

In some places, technicians' work is strenuous. It can also be dangerous. Technicians may be needed at odd hours to respond to emergencies. They often go equipped with hardhats, gloves, and other safety equipment.

Workplace owners and supervisors sometimes frown when health and safety technicians visit. They frequently accuse inspectors of nitpicking when looking for violations. In the long run, though, these technicians benefit employers as well as employees. Ensuring that the workplace is safe and efficient results in fewer employee absences and equipment breakdowns. The

AVOIDING LEGAL ENTANGLEMENTS

If workplace owners and supervisors, government regulators, and inspectors can't prevent on-the-job accidents, thousands of lawyers are eager to address the issues after the fact. Many of the million-plus lawyers in the United States handle personal injury and workers' compensation cases.

Workers who are injured on the job are entitled to have their injuries and related losses paid for. Workers' compensation lawyers make sure that these workers receive all their benefits.

Personal injury lawyers usually represent clients who are injured in homes, in traffic accidents, and in public places. Often they take on cases of clients injured in the workplace. They try to show in court that the accident was caused by the negligence (neglect of safety) of someone (in this situation, the employer). If they succeed, they can win millions of dollars in damages. Even if the defending employer wins the verdict, the legal costs to defend the case may be staggering.

Ensuring health and safety on the job can go a long way toward averting legal quagmires.

risk of lawsuits decreases, and liability insurance rates may drop. By pointing out where the facility is violating government regulations, technicians help the company avoid fines.

Students interested in this career should be proficient in math and science, especially chemistry, physics, and biology. Their job tools will include computers and electronic testing equipment. They should be detail-oriented and should develop problem-solving and communication skills.

Certification isn't required, but many employers favor certified technicians. The Board of Certified Safety Professionals offers three main types: Construction Health and Safety Technician Certification (CHST), Safety Trained Supervisor (STS), and Occupational Health and Safety Technologist Certification (OHST).

PREPARING YOURSELF

Most occupational health and safety technicians are high school graduates who will learn their duties on the job. Some obtain associate's degrees at a community college or online; course subjects include respiratory protection and material storage and handling. All are instructed in laws governing workplace safety and health and inspection methods.

FUTURE PROSPECTS

In the near future, the growth rate for this job market is expected to be about 13 percent (average, in the overall job growth picture), according to the Bureau of Labor Statistics. New environmental laws and regulations will probably be passed, especially in the field of nuclear energy. These additional regulations will call for more technicians to collect and test data.

FOR MORE INFORMATION

BOOKS

Friend, Mark A., and James P. Kohn. *Fundamentals of Occupational Safety and Health*. 5th ed. Lanham, MD: Government Institutes (Rowman & Littlefield), 2010.
This volume provides an overview of modern issues in occupational safety and health.

Goetsch, David L. *Occupational Safety and Health for Technologists, Engineers, and Managers*. 7th ed. Upper Saddle River, NJ: Prentice Hall, 2010.
This book includes in-depth coverage of all aspects of safety and health issues in the workplace.

ORGANIZATIONS

Board of Certified Safety Professionals
2301 W. Bradley Avenue
Champaign, IL 61821
(217) 359-9263
Web site: http://www.bcsp.org
The Board of Certified Safety Professionals provides certification for safety technicians.

Bureau of Labor Statistics (BLS)
Division of Information and Marketing Services
2 Massachusetts Avenue NE, Room 2850
Washington, DC 20212
(202) 691-5200
Web site: http://www.bls.gov
An agency within the U.S. Department of Labor, the
    BLS measures labor market activity, working condi-
    tions, and other economic factors concerning the
    U.S. labor market. Its *Occupational Outlook Hand-
    book* provides career information on hundreds of
    occupations. (See http://www.bls.gov/ooh/
    healthcare/occupational-health-and-safety
    -technicians.htm.)

National Institute for Occupational Safety and Health
    Centers for Disease Control and Prevention
1600 Clifton Road
Atlanta, GA 30333
(800) 232-4636
Web site: http://www.cdc.gov/niosh
The National Institute for Occupational Safety and
    Health is the federal agency responsible for conduct-
    ing research and making recommendations for pre-
    venting work-related injuries and illnesses.

Occupational Safety and Health Administration
U.S. Department of Labor
200 Constitution Avenue NW
Washington, DC 20210
(800) 321-6742
Web site: http://www.osha.gov
This is the federal government agency responsible for
    overseeing working conditions and for ensuring safe,
    healthy environments.

PERIODICALS

Occupational Health & Safety
14901 Quorum Drive, Suite 425
Dallas, TX 75254
(972) 687-6700
Web site: http://ohsonline.com
This publication covers a variety of workplace safety
    and health topics, from confined spaces to fire safety
    to showers and eyewash.

Safety+Health
1121 Spring Lake Drive
Itasca, IL 60143
(800) 621-7619

Web site: http://www.nsc.org/safetyhealth
This magazine is published by the National Safety Council.

APPS AND VIDEOS

"The Principles of Accident Investigation." YouTube upload, February 9, 2010 (http://www.youtube.com/watch ?v=JBa8FRTvqbY&playnext=1&list=PLEC9B227BF 9230238&feature=results_main).
This video depicts the kinds of workplace situations that should be investigated.

SafetyNet (Predictive Solutions)
This app helps users inspect worksites and analyze their observations, allowing them to predict and prevent accidents.

WEB SITES

Due to the changing nature of Internet links, Rosen Publishing has developed an online list of Web sites related to the subject of this book. This site is updated regularly. Please use this link to access the list:

http://www.rosenlinks.com/CCWC/Scien

CHAPTER 13

REAL ESTATE ASSESSORS

Real estate assessors and appraisers determine the value of property. They inspect existing and new properties and estimate the values of the land and the buildings on it. Value estimates are important for sellers and buyers in negotiating prices. This information also determines how much property owners will be taxed and how much insurance is needed.

Appraisers and assessors begin by gathering and verifying information about the property from available sources. These include public property records containing legal descriptions of the property. During on-site inspections, appraisers and assessors make note of special features and take photographs inside and out. They note the general location of the property and research the values of similar property in the area. They also cite specific factors that can affect the value of the property, such as exceptional highway noise and hazards. Structures may be damaged or deteriorating and require repair.

Assessment and appraisal professionals write property value reports, which they keep updated. Their work may involve coding and tabulating numbers.

Obviously, assessors and appraisers must be good at math. They must be able to judge the quality and importance of property and detect problems or possible problems. Other skills that are essential for this work include:

- Analytical skills to weigh and understand all the data they collect about a property
- Organizational and problem-solving skills to see a complex assessment/appraisal project to completion
- Time management skills; assessors and appraisers often evaluate numerous properties in a day and work under deadline pressure

A 1989 earthquake caused this destruction to an apartment complex in San Francisco. Assessors are trained to detect structural and other problems that are much less obvious.

- Social skills for communicating effectively with clients to obtain information and answer questions

Appraisers usually work on one piece of property at a time. Many of them specialize in either commercial property (stores, office buildings) or residential property (houses, apartment buildings).

Assessors sometimes value whole neighborhoods at one time. They do this by using computerized appraisal systems. Most assessors are employed by local governments to help determine the tax values of property. They must be thoroughly knowledgeable of assessment methods. If a property owner challenges the estimated tax value, the assessor will need to verify the accuracy of the assessment.

Some workers, especially appraisers, spend much of their time in their offices. Assessors

An assessor takes notes on the extent and causes of this damaged home ceiling. Some inspectors specialize in a certain category of property—homes, office buildings, or industrial sites.

JOB OPENING: TOWN PROPERTY ASSESSOR

Many property assessors work for small towns and counties. Their reports are essential for determining accurate and fair property taxes.

A typical advertisement for an assessor in a New England town described the following duties:

- Extensive work in the field, analyzing new properties and reviewing existing sites
- Administrative work in the office
- Using independent judgment and following local and state program guidelines in making assessments
- Maintaining printed and computerized records of maps, declared values, road and street details, historic property values and tax rates, and other information

The agency listed no specific academic requirements but wanted candidates with a solid combination of experience and training. The successful job candidate was required to have the assessor's certificate for that state and maintain it with continuing education each year.

also work in offices but spend many hours in the field. Physical requirements include good vision to observe detail.

While some appraisers and assessors have no advanced education, special study is advisable to improve employment and advancement opportunities. Professionals in this area can benefit from courses in finance, math, computer science, and economics. Knowledge of real estate law is also useful.

The use of computers and software for entering and processing data is a regular part of property assessment and appraisal today. Workers use desktop computers in the office as well as notebook computers and personal digital assistants (PDAs) or smartphones in the field. Computer programs are used for mapping, appraising, and analyzing numbers and information. Workers also use handheld gadgets such as digital measuring devices.

PREPARING YOURSELF

State or local governments establish requirements for education and experience for real estate assessors. A high school diploma may be the only requirement. The agency may require assessors to take appraisal courses. On-the-job training may be arranged as part of an apprenticeship.

Appraisers, depending on the class of property they'll be working with, typically must have at least an associate's degree. A few appraisal jobs are open to applicants with only a high school diploma.

Property evaluators must be licensed. Appraisers must obtain certification. Some states also require assessors to obtain certificates. Different levels of certification determine the types of property and maximum property values the worker is qualified to appraise or assess. Appraisers and assessors take continuing education classes to renew their licenses and certificates.

FUTURE PROSPECTS

The need for real estate appraisals and assessments partly depends on the extent of current activity in real estate sales. The market was off dramatically early in the century, with a sluggish rebound. The Bureau of Labor Statistics expects the job growth rate for appraisers and assessors to be only about 7 percent between 2010 and 2020, below the average of occupations generally.

FOR MORE INFORMATION

APPS

Appraisers (mjcapp)
This app includes a directory of residential and commercial property appraisers.

Property Search Organizer (Aykira)
This app provides an easy way to collect and manage property and appraisal details.

BOOKS

Gladwell, Stephen. *Appraisers and Assessors of Real Estate: Job Hunting—A Practical Manual for Job Hunters and Career Changers.* Newstead, QLD, Australia: Emereo Pty Ltd., 2011.
Gladwell provides advice and strategies for interviewing and landing a job as an appraiser or assessor.

Real Estate Essentials. New York, NY: LearningExpress, LLC, 2007.
This study guide and glossary is useful for people interested in a real estate career.

ORGANIZATIONS

Bureau of Labor Statistics (BLS)
Division of Information and Marketing Services
2 Massachusetts Avenue NE, Room 2850
Washington, DC 20212
(202) 691-5200
Web site: http://www.bls.gov
An agency within the U.S. Department of Labor, the BLS
measures labor market activity, working conditions,
and other economic factors concerning the U.S. labor
market. Its *Occupational Outlook Handbook* provides
career information on hundreds of occupations. (See
http://www.bls.gov/ooh/business-and-financial/
appraisers-and-assessors-of-real-estate.htm.)

International Association of Assessing Officers
314 W. 10th Street
Kansas City, MO 64105
(816) 701-8100
Web site: http://www.iaao.org
The International Association of Assessing Officers
provides research and educational information for
government assessment officials.

International Real Estate Institute
P.O. Box 879

Palm Springs, CA 92263
(760) 327-5284, ext. 252; (877) 743-6799
Web site: http://www.irei-assoc.org
This professional organization connects real estate
    professionals with those who require professional
    realty reports.

National Association of Real Estate Appraisers
P.O. Box 879
Palm Springs, CA 92263
(760) 327-5284, ext. 252; (877) 815-4172
Web site: http://www.narea-assoc.org
The National Association of Real Estate Appraisers
    provides updates on guidelines, regulations, and
    trends in the appraisal profession.

WEB SITES

Due to the changing nature of Internet links, Rosen
Publishing has developed an online list of Web sites
related to the subject of this book. This site is updated
regularly. Please use this link to access the list:

http://www.rosenlinks.com/CCWC/Scien

CHAPTER 14

SURVEYING AND MAPPING TECHNICIANS

If you have special interests in measuring distances, drawing diagrams, and/or tramping around outdoors, there are two related career fields to consider. Surveying and mapping technicians help professional surveyors and map makers (cartographers). They are also hired by photogrammetrists, professionals who make photographic (most notably aerial) surveys.

Precision accuracy is critical in this line of work. Surveying and mapping technicians use—and repair or adjust, when necessary—delicate equipment. They work as members of a team, so they have to be able to communicate and cooperate well with others.

If you search the Internet for information about surveying technicians, you may be thrilled by pictures of workers in awesome scenes. You might see them poised at the edge of a precipice, peering through a tripod-mounted leveling scope across a sunbathed canyon. More often in practice, technicians hack through briars and underbrush to find a measuring point in some unglamorous, abandoned property site.

Frequently, surveying technicians work out of sight from others and communicate via mobile devices. They follow careful

Surveyors and their technicians use highly advanced instruments to make exact boundary and distance measurements. Much of their work is done outdoors, sometimes in rugged landscapes.

instructions from their crew chiefs. Often they find themselves isolated from other team members and must make quick decisions on their own.

Those who work outdoors must be physically fit, able to tote equipment across rugged and hilly landscapes, perhaps for miles. They may be on their feet for hours on end. Sometimes they work in adverse weather conditions.

A surveying party is led by a professional surveyor or experienced technician (the party chief). One or more technicians assist. Surveying technicians help take measurements of the land area under study. Their tasks include:

- Going to geographic locations to take surveying measurements and taking notes on features of the site
- Looking for markers noted in older surveys (stones, metal spikes, etc.)
- Operating different surveying instruments to gather data
- Driving stakes and noting permanent landmarks that will be useful in the survey
- Entering survey data into a computer program; some of this data entry may be done on site, some of it in the office

In addition to distances, surveying professionals record elevations and compass directions. This worker is taking measurements at a construction site.

- Helping process the data on returning to the surveyor's office

Mapping technicians do most of their work using computer programs. They help create maps from geographic data collected in the field or by photogrammetry. Mapping technicians perform tasks such as:

- Locating information in computer databases to create a particular map
- Developing maps that show property boundaries, elevations, and geographic features, such as streams and ponds
- Helping cartographers perform future updates to keep maps accurate and reliable

Some mapping technicians work with photogrammetrists. They help fill in the gaps of surveys that are not completely covered by aerial photos. Others specialize in graphic information system (GIS) technology. Obtaining and integrating data from different sources, they assemble and display the results onscreen.

Legal property records must be taken into account with surveys and maps. Technicians sometimes visit courthouses and law firms to check records of property lines and obtain other details.

SURVEYOR WAR STORIES

Surveyors and surveying technicians who work in the field have lots of stories to tell—some funny, some scary.

Greg Johnston, who works with a surveying company in Tampa, Florida, recalls an encounter with an unfriendly dog during a Saturday outing to check boundary markers at a subdivision. Although chained, the dog broke his restraint and kept the surveyors at bay until the owner came to their rescue. (See http://www.youtube.com/watch?v=RrrkTdqvPR0.)

Sean Barron in Gainesville, Florida, tells of the day his equipment was stolen while working at a street site in Miami. While he looked on, a car pulled to a stop and a man jumped out and made away with his entire setup. (Barron got the license number.)

Chris Root, a surveyor in central Florida, reports on an extended project in swamplands, where he and his team were greeted by such natural inhabitants as wild boars, cougars, pygmy rattlesnakes, water moccasins, and a gigantic orb weaver spider. (See http://landsurveyorsunited.com/profiles/blogs/6-weeks-in-the-swamp.)

As more than one surveying technician has remarked, "No two days are the same."

State and local government agencies hire surveying and mapping technicians for highway, zoning, and other projects. Most technicians, though, are employed by surveying, mapping, and engineering firms that serve private property owners or work for the government on contract.

PREPARING YOURSELF

Surveying technicians need only a high school diploma. They learn job skills under the supervision of a licensed surveyor or party chief. Mapping technicians may need to take technical school or community college courses to master graphic information system technology and related subjects.

High school students interested in surveying or mapping should take courses in algebra, geometry, trigonometry, mechanical drawing, computer science, and drafting.

FUTURE PROSPECTS

The Bureau of Labor Statistics projects a growth rate of about 16 percent in the coming years for surveying and mapping technicians. This is about the overall average for projected job growth in all fields. Advances in mapping technology will call for more knowledgeable mapping technicians. Some experienced surveying technicians advance to positions as party chiefs. With further education, they can become licensed surveyors.

FOR MORE INFORMATION

BOOKS

Gladwell, Stephen. *Surveyors, Cartographers, Photogrammetrists, and Surveying and Mapping Technicians.* Newstead, QLD, Australia: Emereo Pty Ltd., 2011.
Gladwell offers advice and strategies for getting a job in this career field.

Petersen, Christine. *The Surveyor* (Colonial People). Pelham, NY: Benchmark Books, 2010.
Petersen provides a historical look at how surveyors worked in the 1700s.

ORGANIZATIONS

American Society for Photogrammetry and Remote Sensing
5410 Grosvenor Lane, Suite 210
Bethesda, MD 20814-2160
(301) 493-0290
Web site: http://www.asprs.org
This society provides certification for photogrammetric technologists and relevant information.

Bureau of Labor Statistics (BLS)
Division of Information and Marketing Services

2 Massachusetts Avenue NE, Room 2850
Washington, DC 20212
(202) 691-5200
Web site: http://www.bls.gov
An agency within the U.S. Department of Labor, the BLS
    measures labor market activity, working conditions,
    and other economic factors concerning the U.S. labor
    market. Its *Occupational Outlook Handbook* provides
    career information on hundreds of occupations. (See
    http://www.bls.gov/ooh/architecture-and-engineering/
    surveying-and-mapping-technicians.htm.)

National Council of Examiners for Engineering and
    Surveying
280 Seneca Creek Road
Seneca, SC 29678
(864) 654-6824, (800) 250-3196
Web site: http://ncees.org
This nonprofit organization is dedicated to advancing
    professional licensing for engineers and surveyors.

National Society of Professional Surveyors
5119 Pegasus Court, Suite Q
Frederick, MD 21704
(240) 439-4615
Web site: http://www.nsps.us.com

The National Society of Professional Surveyors administers a number of certification programs, including that for Certified Surveyor Technician (CST).

North American Cartographic Information Society
P.O. Box 399
Milwaukee, WI 53201
(414) 229-6282
Web site: http://www.nacis.org
The North American Cartographic Information Society is a professional organization for mapping specialists.

PERIODICALS

The American Surveyor
905 W. 7th Street, #331
Frederick, MD 21701
(301) 620-0784
Web site: http://www.amerisurv.com
This publication includes reports on issues and news related to the surveying profession.

Professional Surveyor Magazine
20 W. 3rd Street
Frederick, MD 21701
(301) 682-6101

Web site: http://www.profsurv.com
Articles cover various categories of surveying, including
    aerial mapping.

VIDEOS

"Six Weeks in the Swamp." LandSurveyorsUnited.com
    (http://landsurveyorsunited.com/profiles/blogs/
    6-weeks-in-the-swamp).
This video chronicles a Florida excursion fraught with
    cougar, wild boar, and rattlesnake encounters.

WEB SITES

Due to the changing nature of Internet links, Rosen
Publishing has developed an online list of Web sites
related to the subject of this book. This site is updated
regularly. Please use this link to access the list:

http://www.rosenlinks.com/CCWC/Scien

GLOSSARY

ABSTRACT MATHEMATICS Math that works with theories, not definite numbers.

ADMINISTRATIVE Having to do with the management of an office or business.

AUTOMATION The process by which many copies of a product are produced the same way, using the same production system.

BIODEGRADABLE Capable of being broken down by living organisms and returned to natural states.

BRICK-AND-MORTAR Relating to a physical retail store or other building, rather than an online seller.

CARDIOVASCULAR Relating to the heart and blood vessels.

COLLATERAL An item of property that a borrower legally offers in advance to a lender in case the loan is not paid.

DIGITAL Having to do with numbers; today, the term is used to refer to computer and Internet data.

DRAFTING Drawing plans, sketches, and designs of property and other objects.

ECONOMIC GROWTH The rate of growth of the goods and services a country produces over a period of time.

ECOSYSTEM A community of living and nonliving things, dependent on one another; loosely, a local environment.

GEOGRAPHIC The study of Earth's surface features.

GYROSCOPE A device used for measuring an object's position and bearings.

HYGIENE The practice of maintaining good health.

MASS In scientific terms, a bulky substance.

MECHANICAL DRAWING Drawing a property or other physical object using special instruments.

MICROPROCESSOR The computer part that contains the "guts" of the machine's operations.

ORGANISM A living unit composed of complex, interrelated parts.

PREFABRICATED Assembled before installation; a prefabricated carport is made in a factory, then delivered and installed at a residence.

PROPULSION The act of moving an object forward or backward.

PROSTHETIC A manufactured corrective body part, such as a dental bridge or artificial limb.

TELECOMMUNICATION Communication between points from a distance, as by telephone or satellite technology.

UNDERWRITING Taking responsibility to pay for a loan if the borrower can't pay.

INDEX

ABOUT THE AUTHOR

Daniel McGuinness is a writer who lives in South Carolina. He has written several career-related books for young people, including one on volunteering for teens who like math and science.

PHOTO CREDITS